# The Journey of Spirit Rising

# The Journey of Spirit Rising

## A Commoner's Journey to Uncommon Joy

by
Rev. Paula J. Richards

Editor: Martin J. Coffee

ISBN-13: 978-1495327698
ISBN-10: 1495327698

10 9 8 7 6 5 4 3 2 1

# Dedication

To my dad, Joseph Paul Lemire, who left me his heart of joy.

### Heart of Joy

Story book friends, tales of *Bunny Blue*,
and *So Dear to My Heart*, my memory of you.

Your heart full of joy, love you did sow,
like towers we built high, my pride in you does grow.

Dance to the music, twirl 'cross the floor,
I once was your princess, will be forever more.

A favorite memory, us raking fall leaves,
But spiraling downward now, oh how my heart grieves.

Sadness, be gone! Don't stand in my light.
Dad left me his heart of joy. I will be all right.

*Your loving daughter,*

*Paula*

# About the author

Worn down by her work, and feeling restless and confused about her direction in life, Paula was ready for change. In 1998, she left a secure, twenty-five year nursing career to pursue her rekindled passion for creating art. That step, along with other unconventional choices, gradually ushered in a new role for her. She began working with people of all ages and backgrounds, guiding them through challenging life transitions by helping them live more authentically. An ordained ministerial counselor, Paula founded Spirit Rising Ministries in 2012. Through her spiritual counseling, writing, speaking, and art, and through her life well lived, she is dedicated to helping people remember the joyful, divine truth about themselves. Her greatest fulfillment is empowering people with tools and insights that can help them on their own journey to joy.

# Table of Contents

# Acknowledgements

I would like to begin by thanking an old friend, Mary Webster, for encouraging me to write down the many stories I shared with her about my spiritual journey, and nudging me to weave them together as memoir. Your editing in the early stages helped me find my voice and set the tone for the entire book. Thank you to my friend, Rev. Michael Eaton, for your editorial suggestions and your gentle, loving support during the past few years of our spiritual journey together. Many thanks to Alan Packer for your tremendous editorial guidance. You helped this book shine. Thank you to my friend, Rev. Michael Eaton, for your editorial suggestions and your gentle, loving support during the past few years of our spiritual journey together. Thank you to Rev. Susan Lewis, for helping me to see the light. Also, a big thank you to Jennifer Lord, Andy Kittross, Tracy Marks, Susan Rizzo, Joyce Josephson, Tony Moschetto, Don Yansen, David Price, Michelle Balbat, Michelle Snyder, Courtney Stano, and Michelle Palmer, from my writer's group, for reviewing this entire manuscript with me. Your patience and thoughtful feedback truly helped the story flow and gave me the incentive to continue writing. Thank you to my new friend, Kristen Marcoux, for bolstering my confidence about sharing my spiritual journey with the world. A huge thank you to my professional editor, Martin Coffee, for helping make these pages sparkle and bringing my longtime dream of being published to life.

It is especially true with a memoir that there are many people who have also indirectly contributed to this work. Most obvious, and deeply loved, are my immediate family—my former husband, Roger Richards, and our two sons, Michael and Gregory, our two lovely daughters–in-*love*, Leslie and Kayli, and my brother, David Lemire, and his wonderful family. Overwhelming gratitude to my mom, Verna Lemire, for your unconditional love over the last sixty-two years, even though, at times, I am hard to understand. You are my role model, my anchor, and my best friend. Thank you to my dad, Joseph Paul Lemire, to whom this book is dedicated, for your selfless, shining love while here on earth, and for continuing to guide me ever so gently from above. Heartfelt thanks to John J. Orifice for your love, wisdom, and support through some of the biggest challenges of my life, and for asking the questions that helped clarify the title for this book. My dear friends, Kathy Kliskey Geraghty, Eileen Dern, Susan O'Leary, Susan Webber, and Shirley Hopkins, I can't possibly thank you enough for always believing in me. Without your support, I am not sure I would ever have journeyed to the joy that I have written about, at least not in this lifetime. For my many other friends, too numerous to count, who have blessed my life in so many wonderful ways, my deepest gratitude. You know who you are. Others, whose names were changed for privacy, played a significant enough role in my life to have been included in my story. Thank you. I also want to thank not only all those who have supported me, but those who have challenged me as well. You have been my greatest teachers. Thank *you*, dear readers, for your interest in my work. Let us journey to joy together. Lastly, I thank God for shining His love through all of us as He gently guides us home.

## The Laughing Dragon

Why does the Dragon laugh?
Because it knows things for what they are.
That rumbling you feel - the beginning of laughter?
It's the Dragon waking, fearless and wonderful!
When the Dragon wakes, the Spirit rises.
When the Spirit rises, we are free.

Author Unknown

# Preface

When I was a little girl, my family took a trip from our home in Massachusetts to Canada. I didn't even know what Canada was back then, but I was excited. We left so early in the morning that it was still dark outside. I settled in with my favorite stuffed animal for what I was told would be a very long ride. We had only driven down our short street, across an intersection and up one hill when I popped up from the backseat and chirped, "Are we there yet?"

In my mid-thirties, I found myself still asking the same question. Like my vague concept of Canada many years ago, I didn't quite know where I was trying to get to in my life. I just wanted to know, *was I there yet?* It didn't feel like it.

Although I was married to a wonderful man, with whom I had two children I adored, owned a lovely home, and had a successful nursing career, something still seemed to be missing from this good life. I kept wondering, *what more did I have to offer the world? What was my heart telling me to do? Who was I beyond being a wife, mother, daughter and nurse?* And more importantly, *Why weren't those roles enough?* I was determined to find out.

Thus began my journey. It lasted for many years

and I traveled alone. For a long time, no one even knew I was absent. When people discovered I had gone, they were very surprised, but no one was more surprised than I was. This was not a journey I planned on taking. Instead, the journey seemed to take me.

In order to move forward, there were many things I felt I had to leave behind. At times I felt sad and frightened, but the more steps I took toward uncovering my true self, the happier and more peaceful I became. I discovered that the only thing missing from my life was the joy of knowing the truth that I am One with God. All my searching led me back to myself, where He has always been.

Turns out . . . God was never lost.

I was.

# Tilling the Soil

## 1986—Something Missing

### A Golden Life

I often used to tell my friend that I had a golden life. Sometimes she would just smile, look me in the eye and say, "There's no growth with a golden life." I didn't understand what she meant. At age thirty five, I was about to find out.

I did have a golden life in many ways. I had a romantic, attentive husband; two sons that I adored; loving, supportive parents and strong ties with my brother and our extended family. I was healthy again after a nine-month bout with cancer. I had a rewarding, albeit stressful, nursing career, a small circle of loyal friends and many interesting acquaintances. My family enjoyed a comfortable home and we had enough money to pay our bills and enjoy recreational activities.

Still, something was missing. I knew it seemed like I had it all. For that I was truly grateful. But something was not quite right and I didn't know what it was. I wasn't unhappy. However, I wasn't sure that I was truly happy either. I didn't know what to do about these feelings of emptiness and unrest inside of me. Although

3

I was raised in the Catholic religion, I no longer felt aligned with any particular doctrine that I could turn to for support. In fact, I wasn't sure I believed in anything. Lying in bed one night with vague thoughts of discontent swirling through my head, I searched my mind for answers. I began thinking that, surely, if there was a power greater than myself, it would be able to hear me, whether I knew how to pray or not. So, without knowing to whom or what it was directed, I hopefully whispered a single word—"Help."

It was soon afterward that the unrest with my life led me to pick up a book by motivational author Dr. Wayne W. Dyer. In it he said, "What is *your* passion? What stirs your soul and makes you feel like you're totally in harmony with why you showed up here in the first place? Know this for certain: Whatever it may be, you can make a living doing it and simultaneously provide a service for others. I guarantee it." His words had a strong impact on me. He not only encouraged me to ask myself what it was I liked to do, but he suggested that I could do what I loved in service to others *and* earn a living doing it!

For the first time since I made my career choice seventeen years earlier, I entertained the thought that I could change paths. I put the book down, sat there on my couch and silently asked myself, *Paula, what is it that you love to do?* What came to me was that I loved color. I always noticed and commented on the color of people's clothing. I would tell them, "Oh, I love the color of your blouse!" or "What a beautiful color! That looks great on you." I was fascinated with color. I didn't know what I could possibly *do* with that piece of information. Discouraged, I put the book away and went about my day, but the following morning I awoke with an idea. I remembered reading about a company that was devoted to helping people select clothing and makeup colors that were most flattering to them. *Hmmm. I could be on to something.* Within a few days, I had researched and found a similar company that would soon be offering training in my area. I knew that I was going to need a space to work in and money to purchase my training kit. I got busy cleaning out our designated "junk room" in our finished basement and planned a yard sale to raise the funds I needed.

I was surprised at how quickly I moved forward with this venture. Something about it just felt right. There was a spark of excitement inside me that I hadn't experienced in a long time. For years I had secretly entertained the thought of being my own boss. Could this be my chance? Little did I know that this first baby step, which felt like taking a risk, was only the beginning.

## My First Business

I had watched the UPS truck pass by my house every morning. This day, I was waiting for it to stop at my door. My color analysis kit was supposed to arrive and I couldn't believe how excited I was. Deep down, I sensed that I was onto something big, maybe even life-changing, but I wasn't sure what.

When the kit finally arrived, I opened it with glee and spent hours looking through the color swatches that would help me determine which colors looked best on people. The samples of fabric were approximately fifteen inches square and there were about thirty or so colors for each of the four seasons. They were made to drape over a person's shoulders to see which colors best complemented their hair, skin and eyes. My clients would come downstairs to my studio and sit in front of a large mirror. As I held different shades of fabric next to their face, they would begin to see how much healthier and more alive they looked in certain colors. Sometimes the results were dramatic. It was great fun helping people to look their best and save money by coordinating their wardrobes.

Although I was growing more and more restless with my nursing career, doing something a bit more "colorful" and creative took the edge off my discontent for a while. But work at the hospital was becoming increasingly stressful for me and my business never got off the ground the way I hoped. I enjoyed playing with this venture for over three years, but the color company I worked for became more and more interested in makeup and fashion. That didn't interest me as much. It helped me to polish my personal image, but I can remember telling my husband, "All this makeup and image stuff just isn't me. All I want to do is work with color."

I had no idea that I was so attracted to color because there was an artist in me waiting to emerge. I wasn't aware that every aspect of that business was grooming me for a future role as an artist and business owner. I not only learned how to present myself more professionally, I learned many things about color that an artist needs to know. Later, I would also discover that color has tremendous healing qualities.

# 1990—Enter the Artist

## Impulse

I think it was a growing restlessness with both of my jobs that led me to be uncharacteristically impulsive one day. I had to be at the hospital by 3pm, but I had finished my errands an hour earlier than expected. Normally I would have gone home until it was time to leave for work. Instead, I found myself turning into the parking lot of a group of shops that I had always been meaning to visit. I was both surprised and intrigued to find an artist with his easel set up in the lobby. He was painting an amazingly realistic scene of a young child standing in a meadow. It was charming. I was so fascinated with his beautiful, detailed work that I never even went inside the shops.

Tim was very friendly. We got into such a deep conversation that I almost forgot to go to work. I remember telling him that I felt like I was at a crossroad in my life. I told him how drained I was by my nursing job and that I was looking for a new direction that would still allow me to help people, but in a less stressful environment. I realize now that I was beginning to follow my inner compass. It was no coincidence that one of my first impulses led me straight to an artist.

## The Gift

Not long after I met Tim, another significant event occurred. I had always loved motivational sayings. Sometimes I wanted to have a quote scribed in beautiful, decorative handwriting (calligraphy) to give as a gift, but every time I found a calligrapher whose work I liked, they were either too busy or didn't accept commissions. I mentioned to my mom that I just might have to learn to do it myself. As loving moms often do, she remembered. The following Christmas she presented me with a calligraphy set of my own.

When the holiday rush was over and my two boys were back in school, I found myself spending hours learning how to create beautifully crafted letters. I was fascinated with the simple elegance of the flowing black ink on white paper and the contrast of thick and thin lines that gave striking drama to each word. I wasn't working with color yet, but calligraphy was the most creative thing I had ever done. I was hooked.

At the time, I didn't think of calligraphy as an art form or myself as an artist. In fact, I told my husband that I wished I knew an artist who could draw a portrait of our house so I could make it into a note card and add my calligraphy to it. He responded by saying, "Why don't *you* draw our house?"

"I don't know how to do that. I can't even draw a cube shape!" I exclaimed. I thought that was the end of our discussion, but a while later, my husband showed up with a photograph of our home.

"Here," he said. "Why don't you just trace the outline of the house from this picture and then fill in the details yourself." Well, that didn't seem too threatening. I guessed I could give it a try. And so I tentatively began outlining the image of our house with a pencil.

It looked so promising that I went out the next day and bought a set of drawing pens in a variety of widths. That afternoon, I began filling in the details; cross pieces for window panes, a door knob, bushes, and a tree for added interest. Three hours later, my husband came home from work saying, "Hi honey, how are you? Where are the kids?"

"Kids?" I said. "What time is it?" I had been so absorbed in my work that I completely lost track of the world around me. Fortunately, I managed to scramble around and put supper on the table before too long, but

9

all the while I couldn't get my mind off that drawing. I knew I was on to something important, but I didn't know then that it would totally transform my life.

The following day I went to the local library and borrowed some books on art. I was determined that I would learn how to draw. A few days later I did another pen and ink drawing of a table for two. That evening I sheepishly showed it to my husband. I guess it was pretty good because he took one look at it and said, "You hot shit! (He didn't usually talk like that.) I didn't know you could do this. Where did this come from?" His voice was full of pleasant surprise.

"I really don't know," I replied. I laughingly shrugged it off, but deep inside I was beaming.

**Green Light**

A few weeks later I followed another impulse and found myself stopping at a local gallery and framing shop. I had passed it countless times before, but had never paid it any mind. Not being used to touring galleries, I tentatively stepped inside the front door and made my way through a corridor of lovely paintings. I landed in a room where two women were working together to choose the best mat color to frame a picture. They were trying one mat after another, much the way I had been using fabric color swatches to frame people's faces. I began to see the connection between what I had been doing and where it might be leading me. I also couldn't help but notice – they were having so much fun!

I struck up a conversation with the woman who turned out to be the owner of the shop. In a moment of courage, I decided to show her my recent pen and ink drawing. I don't remember why I had it with me. I think it was sheer awe that I had been able to draw something recognizable! Before she had a chance to comment, my fear got the better of me and I defensively blurted out, "I've never been to art school or anything, and this is only my first drawing." What she said next empowered me. This gracious, talented artist looked me in the eye and said, "Sometimes school can get in the way." That's all she said, but in my heart, I felt I had been given a green light to move forward with my new dream of becoming an artist.

**Joan**

With that encouragement, I decided it was time to find an instructor for private art lessons. Having a young family and still working at the hospital, I didn't have the time or inclination to go back to college, but I did want some help with the basics of drawing. The first person I called was a woman named Joan. I talked to her briefly over the phone and asked about her fees. There was something so compelling about her that it never occurred to me to call anyone else, or even ask to see a sample of her artwork. Joan's voice was soothing and non-judgmental (something of importance to this budding artist). When she spoke, I felt a deep sense of calm and a feeling that all was right with the world.

Classes consisted of small groups of three or four people who met in Joan's home. We sat around a sturdy, oversized, picnic-style table that she had custom made from an incredibly thick slab of wood. It was big and strong enough to take whatever mess we dished out. That huge, empty space beckoned us to dive in to the creative process. I loved sitting at that table.

Joan offered a nice mix of structured lessons on drawing technique and open classes where we could work on whatever we wanted. This gave me the discipline I needed combined with the freedom to explore. I was surprised one day when friends of my family asked me to do a pen and ink portrait of their home. That was a big challenge for me. It took me a very long time to finish the drawing, but I didn't charge them extra for all the hours I spent in the learning process. They were quite pleased with my work and that led to other commissions. I would say "Yes" to a client's request and then run to Joan for help accomplishing whatever I had promised them I would do. Thankfully, she always came through. It kept me challenged and moving forward with my dream.

I once heard an artist say that you haven't truly seen an object until you have tried to draw it. Sure enough, it was after I began drawing likenesses— seeing the light and shadows, the contrast, the delightful mix of colors reflecting off nearby objects, the exquisite beauty of a rusted piece of metal or an old, rundown shack—that I began to view life through new eyes. I was beginning to see myself differently as well.

I was in my own world when I was drawing or painting. Creating art had a meditative effect that helped me quiet my mind. I always felt more peaceful after spending time in my studio. I also felt more and more empowered as my ability to create beautiful paintings increased. I was not only having fun and getting attention for my work, I had found something special that I could call my own. I still wasn't sure just how I would serve humanity, but I finally understood what Pat B. Allen said so eloquently in her book, *Art is a Way of Knowing*, "We owe it to the world to be as alive as we can, to give what is unique in us to give. Art is a way of knowing our gift and learning how to give it."

**A Change of Heart**

Joan ran another business out of her home called Intuitive Inclinations. At first it was of little interest to me. When I would tell people about her, I would say, "She is my art teacher and there's this other thing that she does on the side." It turned out that the *other thing* she did was an extremely important part of who she was. In most everything that Joan did, she trusted her own "intuitive inclinations" and she had created a beautiful, meaningful life for herself. She was like a magnet for people who were looking for advice on how to improve their lives. Through her own life well lived, I could see that she profoundly affected many people she came in contact with, most notably myself. Invariably, during art lessons, discussions about life would arise. While drawing and painting in the calm, meditative space in her home, I was slowly, but surely, absorbing some of her wisdom. I was learning how to listen to my own inner voice. I learned that I *had* an inner voice! Joan not only taught me about art, she helped me to know more about who I was and how I wanted to live my life. I was discovering that I wanted to live by a different set of guiding principles and that there was more to life than what I could detect with my five senses.

These thoughts were still very much in their infancy when my dad died in September of 1990 at the age of 69. He had suffered a stroke many years earlier that mostly affected his ability to speak. In the few days before his passing he had become bedridden and was being cared for at home by my mom. Dad had been in and out of consciousness for a day or so and, on the morning of his passing, he had become unresponsive. My mom needed to go to the store, so I said I would sit with him. While she was gone I sat and held his hand. I talked to him a little, hoping he could hear me. When I stood up and walked to the foot of his bed, I was totally surprised to see my dad open his eyes and look straight

14

at me. He held me transfixed with a clear and remarkably lucid gaze and the most amazing, loving smile I had ever seen. It was as if he knew a beautiful secret and he was trying to tell me something wonderful. His look of deep peace and joy conveyed to me that he was aware of something very beautiful, probably more beautiful than anything he had ever seen or experienced on this earth.

It was months later before I gave myself time and permission to grieve the loss of my dad. I wrote a poem entitled *A Heart Full of Joy* to express the deep connection I had with him. It ends with, "Sadness be gone. Don't stand in my light. Dad left me his heart of joy. I will be all right." But, the sadness did not go away. The joy was harder and harder to find. I wanted to blame this solely on my father's passing, but knew in my heart that there was something deeper going on. I began taking long walks with our dog late at night. I let the darkness envelope me and the stillness allowed me to think. I could retreat from the busy, daytime world of things to do and people to talk to and be alone with my thoughts.

While walking, my thoughts took me to a poem I had written years ago for my husband on our fifteenth anniversary. It ended with, "My heart has always followed yours. I know it always will." I recalled that, after writing that line, I had been shocked to hear my inner voice ask, "Will you?"

"Of course I will!" I replied. *Where did THAT come*

*from?* I thought. After all, I was happily married and Roger was so good to me. We had shared so much together, including raising two wonderful children. Many people used to comment on what a great couple we were and that they could see we had a beautiful life. Leave him? For what? What a ridiculous notion. Slam the lid down on *that* idea! What was I thinking?!

I was thinking *I'm not happy anymore. Even though everything looks perfect, something is missing.*

To insulate myself from the pain of losing my dad and to escape from dealing with these scary new thoughts about my marriage, I turned my attention to another drama in my life. My dad's passing occurred on our youngest son's first day of kindergarten. When Greg came home to find that his Grampy was gone, I believe, in his young mind, that he equated going to school with losing someone you love. My son who so eagerly went to school and enjoyed the first day became terrified about going back. His teacher kept telling me that I had to help him "let go of the apron strings," but I was certain that this was not a simple case of my being overprotective. My happy little boy had become a screaming, crying wreck. Peeling his little fingers off of doorknobs while he shrieked, kicked, wailed and clung to them for dear life became the morning torture session for both of us as I attempted to get him to school. This was TOTALLY out of character for him. I was so concerned for his emotional wellbeing that I feared he would have a mental breakdown. At a loss for what to do, I allowed him to stay home from school for almost two weeks. In the meantime, I was getting feedback and advice on many fronts; from my husband, my mom, teachers and well meaning friends. None of their advice was helping me or my son. The pressure I felt from them to be a disciplinarian and force him to go to school was overwhelming. No one seemed to sense the seriousness of the situation.

After a while, I simply stopped talking to everyone about the problem. I stopped telling them how Greg was doing and defending how I was handling the situation. I, essentially, took things into my own hands. Following my intuition, I found a new school where I felt they were better equipped to help him through this crisis in a calm and loving manner. His new teacher was much more sensitive to the situation and I was forever grateful for how she helped him integrate back into school. Dealing with a situation that challenged my maternal instincts had given me the courage to stand up and do what I felt was best for my son, without caring what anyone else thought. It was a big step for me and prepared me for bigger decisions to come.

After my dad passed, it seemed only natural to begin re-examining my place in the world. I also began to see my mother in a new light. I saw how strong and independent she had become during the last few years of his illness. I watched as she made her way in the world on her own. To me, she appeared to be a tower of strength. As I watched her living alone, questions began forming in my mind. *What would it be like if I were living on my own? Who would I be? Would I still have the same interests and the same friends? Who was I when I was not a wife, mother, daughter or nurse?* At first it was just a mild curiosity, but the need to find out would eventually become a screaming obsession.

## Five Years Simmering

Not ready to explore those questions, I chose to completely ignore them. For the next five years, I immersed myself in developing my artwork. I created a small business called Letters and Lines which consisted of commissioned calligraphy work embellished with pen and ink drawings.

I was quite surprised when the wife of one of the doctors I used to work with commissioned me to do some work for her. I was even more surprised when her husband was the one who came to pick up the order. He was one of the people I had clashed with the most at the hospital. The day before he came to get the invitations, I had been on an unusually energetic cleaning streak. My home was not only spotless, it was "party ready"! There were fresh flowers on the table and candles lit everywhere on the day he arrived. I have no idea why. I did not know he was coming and there was no special event planned. I was simply enjoying my home and who I was becoming as an artist and business person. I guess I was feeling like I was "in my element." It was extremely gratifying to have him see me that way. I'm sure I exuded a calm confidence that he had never seen in me at work. He was quite gracious. Before he left, he thanked me and muttered something under his breath about having been "an old goat" in the past. I knew he was doing his best to apologize and I accepted it as such. It was very healing for me.

In Joan's classes, I had begun exploring other art mediums as well. My first choice was colored pencils. They seemed to be the next logical step in adding color in a way that still gave me lots of control and the ability to do fine detail. It was a couple of years before I decided to give painting a try. My work was a reflection of how I viewed myself at that time; small, tight and controlled. When I brought my first paintbrush to class, I was surprised that Joan didn't laugh me right out of the room. The brush was so small you couldn't see the hairs on it from more than two feet away! Gracious, as always, she didn't laugh. She let me find out for myself that I needed a bigger brush if I wanted to paint anything other than eyelashes.

The first time I used a slightly bigger brush I was shocked. Unlike colored pencils, I discovered that, with paint and lots of water, I could make large washes of color quickly and easily. Even though I was still using very subdued colors and working relatively small, it felt very freeing to me at the time. Joan used to joke that she needed to turn me into "a loose woman".

As I gained more confidence, I began exploring other mediums and entering some of my work in local art shows. I was beginning to see myself as an artist and joined a local art society. There, I reconnected with Tim, the artist I had seen painting outside the gift shop. His detailed, realistic artwork was absolutely incredible to me. I was in awe of his talent, so I was shocked when the judges at a local Fourth of July show selected one of my paintings over his. Mine was an impressionistic rendering of a window with a candle perched on the sill. Because it was not as realistic as Tim's, I believed that my work wasn't as good. Even though I felt that way at the time, the win did a lot to boost my self-confidence.

As my artwork became a bit bigger, bolder and more colorful over the next few years, I was changing too. Calligraphing motivational sayings and creating house portraits was no longer enough. I only did commissioned work on and off for a few years because I believed that I wouldn't reach the full potential of my creative expression by drawing what someone else wanted me to draw. I knew my inspiration had to come from within if I was to be successful. For some artists, commissions are a perfect fit, but it was not the vision I had for myself. I knew there was more, much, much more that I was meant to be doing with my life. Even though I didn't know exactly what it would be, I believed that art would somehow play a role.

I was also beginning to be increasingly aware of

being guided in my life. I was becoming particularly aware of my father's presence. Sometimes, if I experienced a meaningful coincidence or had a moment of insight, my dad would come to mind and I would have the distinct feeling that he was guiding my thoughts or watching over me. One example was when I was helping my mom hang new curtains in her bedroom. I was having trouble driving a screw into the window casing. My dad had been a carpenter, so I silently began asking him to help me. I suddenly remembered that he used to start the hole with a nail first. Just as I had that thought, my mom said, "Your father used to start the hole with a nail first." I smiled to myself and finished hanging the curtains without any more problems. I was not always sure that dad was really helping me, but I did find the thought comforting.

# 1995—A Greater Plan

## My Sacred Self

After five years of what I came to view as "art therapy" with Joan, I was beginning to listen more to my inner voice. The sense of being guided was getting stronger. One day I awoke with the distinct feeling that I was supposed to go to the bookstore. The thought came from "out of the blue," a sign that I would later recognize more clearly as guidance. There was no particular book that I had in mind to buy at that time, but I decided to follow my *inclination* and go to Borders Bookstore. I went to the New Age section which was fast becoming my favorite. I especially enjoyed reading books by Dr. Wayne W. Dyer. I searched the shelves for a very long time. There were many interesting books, but none seemed to jump off the shelf. I finally gave up, thinking, *This whole inner guidance thing is just something I made up. It's not real.* I was disappointed and frustrated.

As I turned toward the exit, I walked directly into a huge, free standing display of Dr. Wayne Dyer's newly published book, *Your Sacred Self, Making the Decision to be Free.* Instantly, I knew that this was the book I had come for. The last time I read one of his books was quite a few years earlier. It was *You'll See It When You Believe It.* I had always enjoyed everything he had written. I liked that one too, except he had started suggesting more spiritual concepts that I was having trouble understanding, such as manifesting material objects almost instantly by focusing his thoughts on them. But now, five years later, I was ready and here was his new book. It promised to teach me how to tap into the power of my higher self and live each day with a greater sense of peace and fulfillment.

My faith restored, I happily bought the book and returned home. I devoured the whole thing in just two days, but it would take the next few years for me to begin incorporating its message into my life. Through his teachings, Dr. Dyer helped me to understand that I am a spiritual being having a human experience. Also, that we each have a unique life purpose and it is extremely important for us to discover and honor whatever that purpose is. I became more and more convinced that there was a greater plan in store for me than what I was currently living.

# 1998—I Believe I Can Fly

**Excitement vs. Fear**

It was this strong belief in a grander and more purposeful life, coupled with increasing anxiety in regards to my work demands at the hospital, that led me to take a huge leap of faith. It happened after I had taken a two-week vacation from work. That was the first time in many years that I had been away from the hospital setting for more than a few days at a time. When I returned, the crushing weight of responsibility and discontent with my job hit me with such force that I could hardly breathe.

I was a registered nurse in the obstetrical department of a local hospital. Helping to bring babies into the world was joyous, but there was also a lot of stress for me. This included a constant struggle in my professional relationships with many of the physicians. This mostly revolved around the fact that I didn't have the confidence to stand up for myself. So, at times, I became an easy target for thinly disguised verbal abuse. It had begun to take its toll.

Maternal/Child Health was the only kind of nursing I had ever wanted to do. I knew this very early on in my studies, so I convinced my employer to let me work in the high-risk obstetrical area without the benefit of some basic medical-surgical experience first. Because I had very limited experience in specialty areas like obstetrics as a student, this turned out to be a poor career move. I found myself much too quick to believe I was wrong if someone told me I was, even though it wasn't always true. This happened quite often and quickly eroded what little confidence I might have had.

I often felt like a small child trying to live in an adult world. Having grown up in a loving and protective home, I struggled with being in an atmosphere where acceptance was based on how well one did one's job, rather than just how nice you were. Of course, that made sense, and I was a hard worker, but not necessarily the most skilled one, especially in the beginning. By the time my skills had improved, my confidence had already been shaken so badly that I just couldn't seem to recover.

I also struggled with something that I couldn't even admit to myself for almost another twenty years. The truth was that I didn't like practicing medicine. I had loved working as a nurse's aide many years before. I thought becoming a nurse would be like a glorified aide's position. It wasn't until my junior year in college that I began to see what I had gotten myself into. The realization of the enormous increase in responsibility totally overwhelmed me. There was so much to learn and I wasn't even sure if I cared about any of it. All I knew was that I wanted to help people. I loved to comfort and reassure people when they were scared and I was very good at it. Even happy, pregnant patients were often frightened, so it seemed like the place for me to be. But learning about the liver, spleen and kidneys or how to resuscitate someone or operate IV pumps and other mechanical devices—none of this interested me. Because I didn't know what else to do, I struggled on with my education and, ultimately, with my entire career.

The biggest threat to my ego came just three years after I graduated from nursing school. My husband had begun working as an orderly two years earlier and came home one day announcing that he was going to get his nursing degree. Because he was extremely smart and science oriented, I knew he would learn medicine easily. I was terrified that he would soon find out what a fraud I was.

I was so hard on myself back then and had such a distorted view of my abilities. But Roger never questioned my abilities and always showed respect for the different skill set that I had from his career in cardiac care. But we did joke about it when my mom would call with a medical question that didn't involve pregnancy because she would say, "Oh yeah, I forgot, you need to put the *doctor* on the phone." And, indeed,

Roger could easily have been a doctor, but he never wanted to be. He enjoyed being at the patient's bedside and instructing other nurses in cardiac care. He was great at his job, so it took me over twenty years to finally find the courage to admit to him, and more importantly to myself, how I felt about my own career.

I have to say, in my own defense, that I *did* have many wonderful moments during my twenty-five years as a nurse. As time passed, I became much more skilled. Many times I averted life and death situations because of my knowledge and observations. I was often praised by my patients for the wonderful care I gave them. There were many times when I was confident and sure of my abilities and decisions. I felt proud to be doing such wonderful work.

I absolutely loved the psychological aspect of nursing. If someone was in pain, sad or frightened, I would shine. I was able to comfort them and put them at ease. I knew how to explain things simply and clearly so they could better understand and cope with what was going on. There was nothing like having the relative of a patient in crisis stop me in the hall, clasp their hands over mine, look at me through tearful eyes, and say, "We will never forget what you did for us today." In fact, that was my biggest concern about leaving it all behind. I feared that I would never be able to find another avenue where I could help people in such a meaningful way.

But through it all, I couldn't stop focusing on the

times when I felt that I didn't measure up; when mistakes were made; when I felt I could have done more . . . done better. I was constantly beating myself up.

## Leaving nursing

Once I became clear about leaving nursing, an interesting opportunity arose. It wasn't until much later that I would recognize this pattern of having to let something go in order to make space for something new. While attending an art class, I was told of a new art supply store opening near my house. I was so intrigued that I stopped there on my way home from the class.

I immediately fell in love with the store. It had formerly been a showroom for selling camping and hiking gear. The second and third stories were open, loft-like spaces suspended in the center of the store with exposed wooden beams around the perimeter where they used to hang canoes and such. It was spacious, rustic and charming. If it hadn't been located in a retail district, it would have made an awesome home.

I briefly spoke to a young woman employee and scheduled an interview with the owner for two days later. During those two days, excitement and fear waged a constant battle in my mind. I was able to find comfort with the thought that I would keep my job at the hospital by working one day a week, while I tried my new position at the art store on for size. Although I desperately wanted to leave nursing, that would give me the security to do an about face if the new job didn't work out. It would also be less stressful financially.

My interview went very well. The owner said he expected to hire me, but out of fairness, he had one other interview to complete that same afternoon. He said he would call me within two hours. I was really excited until I asked him about the hours. He said, "The position is full-time." That shot a big hole in my security plan! It meant I would have to make a total break from nursing. My fear skyrocketed. What was I getting myself into? I was *not* a person who made change easily. I had worked at the same job for twenty-five years! I didn't know anything about retail. I didn't know that much about art supplies either. I had only dabbled with a few products. For me, this job would be like landing on a different planet.

I went home to wait for the phone to ring. It took the owner four hours to call. That was probably a good thing because I spent the first two hours worrying and thinking about all the reasons why I couldn't make this change. If he had called sooner, I probably would have turned down the position. But gradually my excitement began to take hold. Over those last two hours, it grew like wildfire. I would later come to recognize that if my excitement outweighed my fear by even just a little bit, it was probably safe to move forward with a big decision. I began pacing back and forth, back and forth, in my kitchen. With each step I was more and more certain that I wanted the job. In fact, I realized that I wanted that job with my whole heart and soul. Deep down I knew it wasn't just a job. It was a major leap into my future. By the time the owner called with the offer, I was ready with a resounding "YES!"

I left the hospital in August of 1998. I didn't know exactly how I would feel about it. I knew I would miss my co-workers and friends of course, but I hadn't anticipated the reaction I would receive from them. Beyond their sadness at seeing me leave, many of them seemed upset that *they* weren't the ones leaving. A few joked about it, but some spoke openly about their feelings. At the time, I didn't have the emotional strength to actively encourage them to follow their own dreams. It was all I could do to muster the courage to follow my own.

I felt a little shaky on that last day, but mostly I think I was numb. I had just stepped off a cliff and had no idea if I would land safely or be smashed against the rocks. Many people thought that I could just go back to nursing if the art job didn't work out. They would say, "What is the big deal?" But I knew in my heart that wasn't an option for me. That career had taken too much of a toll on me. Although I only worked two evenings a week, the job felt all consuming. If I were to survive emotionally, I knew I would have to leave nursing behind. I would be working full-time at the art store, and earning $100 less per week, but the tremendous relief I felt at finding the courage to get out of nursing and follow my heart made it all worthwhile.

The morning after accepting the new job, it seemed as if a huge boulder had been lifted off me. I felt joyfully free and ready to face the future, no matter what. At the same time, however, I knew deep down that I was running away from something. Even though I was certain I had made the right choice to leave nursing, the uneasy relationships that I had with many of the doctors over those twenty-five years had not been resolved. I knew that the issue of learning to stand up for myself would eventually come back to challenge me in some other form.

**Mars Landing**

Working at the art supply store was a little like landing on an alien planet. For every product that was familiar to me, there were a hundred others that were not. For the first week or so I worked with the female employee I had met that first day. After that I was mostly left on my own. This was *not* what I had in mind. What did I know about selling anything? And I knew *nothing* about computers except how to send an e-mail. Most of my support came over the phone from people working in the primary store which was over an hour's drive away. Fortunately for me, but not for the business, there were very few customers coming through, so I didn't have to work very fast. It was a new store in an out of the way location and the owner was putting almost nothing into advertising. I got the distinct feeling that this entire job situation was priming me for being *on my own* in a much bigger way.

The most wonderful thing about working there was meeting the customers. It seemed like every person who came into the art store became my friend. There was an instant connection between us that was much deeper than I had ever experienced. Friendships that used to take years to develop were happening almost overnight. I found us having deep, poignant discussions about the meaning and beauty of life and I loved it. I may not have known much about retail, but I had finally discovered a social circle where I fit in. My mind, body and spirit breathed a collective sigh of relief.

Another wonderful thing I discovered also came as a complete surprise to me. Other than my husband, most of the men I had dealt with in my life were doctors who were my superiors and of a much different temperament than me. Now, I was meeting people who viewed the world more creatively and they were my peers, my equals. I soon had more male friends than women. I began to realize that I loved men!

As for the staffing dilemma, the store owner finally hired two other people to work with me; a young man and woman in their twenties. They ended up being two of my greatest teachers, but not in the way I had expected. As it turned out, they had no retail experience either, but it didn't seem to faze them. While I was still excusing my ineptness by telling customers, "I'm new here," the two of them were, in my opinion, bold as brass. Listening to them talk, you would have thought they owned the business. They could talk to customers about *anything*. Name any product and they would tell you all about it. There's a term for people who can do that without any knowledge to back them up, but I'll refrain from using it here.

Of course, one of the people they talked to was my boss. When I finally received my first evaluation, I was shocked to find out that my job was on the line due to my "lack of confidence." I walked out of the meeting reeling with disbelief. Once I calmed down and took a hard look at the situation, I realized that I had put myself in the position of "new kid on the block" once again. I was feeling stressed out, just like I had been in my early days of nursing. The first thing I had to do was get some perspective. No one was going to die if I made a mistake in an art supply store! I realized I had a choice. I could continue with my old way of handling things and let my insecurities get the better of me or I could find my inner strength and move forward with my life.

I gave myself one day off to have a pity party. I cried, on and off, all day. I curled up in a ball and rocked back and forth. I told myself I was a wimp. I worried that my lack of confidence would haunt me forever.

Then, at the end of that day, I told myself to GET OVER IT! The following morning I put on a bold, bright red blouse, applied makeup, which I didn't usually wear, took a deep breath, and squared my shoulders. As I stepped into the store, I vowed to myself that I would never again say, "I'm new here." Instead I would play a game with myself to see how many customers I could serve on my own before needing to call for help. As soon as someone walked in the door, I made eye contact with them and gave them a look that said, "I am here to help you and I can!" Essentially, I faked it 'til I made it.

Of course, my work improved tremendously. Shortly after that, the other two employees left. Their extremely bold, confident demeanor was in such sharp contrast to mine that I think it forced me to work on my confidence level. In contrast, the next employee hired was quick to sing my praises. I received a glowing evaluation from my boss. In truth, neither evaluation was completely accurate. I had merely been shown two extremes; fear and lack of confidence vs. healthy self-confidence and self-respect. It was a major turning point for helping me move toward the person I wanted to become, but I still had a long way to go.

## Nova Scotia

The year I worked at the art store also marked the twenty-fifth anniversary of my marriage to Roger. It was a beautiful marriage and I would have made the same choice all over again. He was loving, attentive, kind, gentle, warm, witty and very romantic. He was also my rock. In many ways, Roger took care of me. But what happened back in 1981 made me less, rather than more, dependent upon him.

I was diagnosed with a cancerous condition known as a "molar pregnancy." The cells that should have formed the placenta began to grow quickly in an abnormal pattern that would not support the fetus' growth and development. My abdomen expanded rapidly, but there was no baby there. I went from being excited about having a child to fearing for my life. After minor surgery to clean out my uterus, six months of chemotherapy and three more months of recuperation, I was finally strong enough to return to work. I found it interesting that my illness lasted exactly as long as a full-term pregnancy would have. I think, subconsciously, I needed to complete that nine-month cycle, even if it was suffering through an illness rather than having a baby. To me, that is a testament to just how powerful the mind can be.

Towards the end of that nine-month ordeal, while curled up on the couch with Roger, he told me,

"The girl that I married needed to be taken care of. The woman I am sitting next to now does not." He saw this long before I actually felt it. I had become so independent over the years that now, seventeen years later, I was entertaining the thought of moving out on my own. Roger had always supported and encouraged me to be my own person. In hindsight, we would end up saying, half joking, half sad, that he had done too good a job.

It wasn't my growing sense of independence, however, that was prompting me to consider moving on. It was all those questions about who I would be *on my own*. I had chosen to ignore them for a long time, but they were resurfacing and it was getting more and more difficult to hold them down. In the 47 years of my life, I had only been on my own for two nights, total. One of those nights was about six years earlier when Roger took our boys on a camping trip. They planned to be away for two or three nights, but it rained so hard that they came home the very next afternoon.

I was shocked at how intense my reaction was when they returned. I tried hard not to let my disappointment show, but it was clearly evident to Roger that I was extremely upset by their early return. He kept apologizing and saying, "We'll stay out of your way and try to give you some space." I thanked him for his concern and caring, but in my mind I just kept screaming, *You don't understand! That's not the same as being ALONE!* My reaction was a strong indicator of just how long and hard I had stuffed down my own needs and desires.

I had gone straight from my parent's home to college to marriage. I was almost always *with* someone. I wanted to develop a better sense of who I was as an individual. Discovering the artist in me was a big step in that process. Finding the courage to leave nursing eight years later was another crucial step. But, through all these changes, I was opening up to a new, more spiritual view of life that no one in my family seemed to share. Although I was still *with* someone most of the time, I often felt more alone than ever. My curiosity about what it would be like to be on my own, and my need to grow, change and explore life in a different way was getting stronger.

For an anniversary gift, my mom offered us a trip. We decided to go to Nova Scotia. I didn't know what my husband's expectations were, but I had a clear agenda. I was going to put my heart and soul into our marriage on that trip. I would give it everything I had to see if I could make it work. I did give it my all, but to no avail.

For the last few years, Roger and I had fallen into a rut of not going out and doing things together. He mostly wanted to stay home, so I was very excited to be traveling with him. Out in that beautiful, scenic playground of nature, I felt joyously free. I found the drive along the coast road exhilarating. With the sun in my face and the wind in my hair, I was in heaven. I approached everything we did with wild abandon and we had a wonderful vacation. I discovered that I still loved Roger immensely, but it was more like the love for a lifetime friend. It wasn't a romantic love anymore. Although I cared very deeply for him and still felt a powerful connection because of all we had shared, I could see us growing further and further apart.

About a year later, the well-known news co-anchors, Chet Curtis and Natalie Jacobson, announced their separation. In a *Boston Globe* newspaper article, an undisclosed friend of Natalie's said, "She was looking for mountains to climb. He was looking for valleys to rest in." I felt that was a good description of my marriage. I knew I would eventually have to move on.

Much later, we attended some family therapy sessions to help our son, Greg, who still lived at home, through our separation. It was there that I admitted that our trip to Nova Scotia was the point when I knew for sure that I had to leave. Sadly, Roger would say that it was the point in our relationship when he had "never loved me more." The shock I felt when he said that nearly knocked me off my chair. I explained to him that what he loved about me on that trip was how free and adventurous I felt. I was thrilled to be out exploring and living life with him more fully than we had done in years.

Gradually, over the years, he had become less and less interested in going places. He said that everything he needed and wanted was right there in our home with me. I loved being in our home with him too, but staying there all the time felt very limiting to me. Perhaps it was because my romantic love for him was waning that we couldn't work this out, but I knew I didn't want to wait and hope for a weeklong adventure once every two or three years. I needed to live life now! I didn't want to be traveling all the time. I just wanted to get out and explore; visit a new town, try something different, climb a hill, watch a sunset, visit friends, go for a walk by the ocean. I did all those things, but I did them alone.

## Time to Say Goodbye?

I began doing everything alone. My art studio became my sanctuary. I used the space not only for painting, but for working through my feelings and planning my future. Although I had not yet found the courage to even dare say I was leaving, I was already shopping at yard sales and picking up small household items I thought I would need. My family always respected the privacy of my studio, so it was easy to store things in my closet without being questioned.

As always, my state of mind was influencing my artwork as well. One of my most successful paintings was one I painted with great passion to the song, "Time to Say Goodbye" sung by Andrea Bocelli and Sarah Brightman. The lyrics weren't in English so I didn't know their meaning, but the music had a heart wrenching quality that deeply moved me. I painted a birch tree and full moon against a dark sky with the silhouette of a bird in flight in front of the moon. Though unintentional, the bird, depending on how you viewed it, looked like it could be coming or going. I felt that it reflected my own wavering between staying in my marriage and leaving. I initially titled the painting "Goodbye." Later, when I was ready to move out, I retitled it "A Wing and A Prayer." When I finally placed it for sale, it sold within a few days. It was my fastest and highest priced sale ever.

My other sanctuary was outdoors, late at night. I was still taking long walks with our big, black Labrador retriever, Cobalt. Sometimes I would walk for an hour or more. I desperately wanted to be alone with my thoughts. As I walked, I would give myself pep talks by singing out loud. My favorite song was "I Believe I Can Fly" by R. Kelly. It spoke of seeing myself running through an open door, spreading my wings and flying away.

Another favorite was "One Way Ticket" by LeAnne Rimes, about stepping into the unknown and starting over again.

I was also beginning to have what seemed to be prophetic dreams that showed me helping a lot of people. In one dream, I was sitting on a rubber raft in the middle of a turbulent sea. All around me were other people on rafts. They were losing their oars, tipping over, and falling off, but my raft and the water surrounding it were very calm. I was instructing everyone else how to steady their rafts.

One of my most powerful dreams came soon after my Uncle Russ died. I dreamt that he and my aunt were sitting in lawn chairs at the end of a grassy field that looked like a runway. They were watching me fly a one person plane like the barnstormers used to fly. I was flipping the controls this way and that, causing the plane to tilt and swerve and do loop-de-loops. But, no matter what I did, the plane would always right itself and come in for a smooth landing. My uncle looked at my aunt, pointed directly into the sky, and said, "He is in charge now. It doesn't matter what Paula does. She will always land on her feet." I believed that my beloved uncle was telling me, from the higher perspective of the spirit world, that it was safe for me to take the risks I was planning on taking.

The more dreams I had, the more motivational songs I heard and articles I read, the more certain I became that there was something else I was supposed to do with my life. I wasn't sure exactly what, but I strongly believed I couldn't find out unless I followed my heart. My heart kept saying *move on*. But the anguish of knowing that my leaving would hurt Roger and so many other people haunted my every waking moment. I prayed constantly, asking the same question over and over again. *Please God, how can I follow my heart and not hurt the people I love?*

One day my friend gave me a gift certificate for a Polarity session which, I was told, was a healing session to help balance the flow of energy in my body. At one point during the treatment, it felt like there was a gentle flow of something coming right in through the top of my head. It wasn't scary or uncomfortable, but it was like nothing I had ever experienced. After the session, the practitioner told me that what I felt was energy coming into my body. Then she completely surprised me by saying that she had sensed a spirit's presence in the room during my session. She said the woman was small, kind of eccentric, and wore a wide brimmed, gardening hat. Her name was Clara and she wanted to know, *How many times was I going to ask the same question?!*

I burst out crying and told the practitioner how sad and scared I was about wanting to leave my husband. She was the first person to ever suggest that my leaving, even though it seemed so hurtful at the time, might be beneficial to my family in ways I couldn't yet imagine. Also, that it was important for me to follow what my heart was calling me to do. She at least partially answered my question right then and there, but it would be years before I finally recognized the answer for myself and, more importantly, believed that it was true.

# 1999—Hardly Breathing

## Breaking the News

I had been through some hard times; lost my dad; survived cancer; but nothing could have prepared me for the anguish of telling my husband that I wanted to leave. I didn't have a plan for when or how to tell him. I was waiting for the "right" moment to present itself. It came unexpectedly one morning when he approached me lovingly and, once again, I pushed him away.

"Do you still love me?" he asked.

"Oh yes!" I replied, "But," I continued, "I'm not sure it's a romantic love anymore."

Silence . . .

Tears blurred my vision, but not before I saw the look of shock register in his eyes.

My heart was pounding so hard that I was sure it could be felt through our neighbor's floorboards.

Always being a man of action in a crisis, Roger momentarily tucked his feelings away and let his first response be a rational one. "We need to tell Greg," he said. He went on to say with a sense of urgency that we needed to call this one and that one and do this and do that. It was all about taking action. I believe he needed to do something, anything, to keep busy in an attempt to hold his world and his emotions together. Trying to assuage his pain and keep him from actually picking up the phone, I began saying that maybe I just needed some time to be on my own for a while. I didn't need to leave right away, but I think we both knew in that moment that, if I left, I would not be coming back.

If you've ever watched science fiction television, you've probably seen them use a transporter. They step on a launch pad and their bodies seem to disintegrate and then materialize somewhere else. That morning I felt like I had stepped on that pad and my body was disintegrating. The problem was, I didn't know where, when, or even *if* it would reappear. I simply felt shattered. My heart lay in sharp edged splinters on the floor, drowning in a pool of salty tears. My pain wasn't just for myself; it was from believing that my husband was shattered too. Watching him sit in silence, staring out the living room window for hours with blank eyes was unbearable. The guilt I felt at abandoning this loving, attentive man who had always been faithful to me simply couldn't be put into words. A few days later Roger told me, "Be very sure this is what you want. I won't risk having you come back and then possibly leave a second time."

At the art store where I worked, there was a young man who used to stop in frequently and hang out. Occasionally we would talk, but most of the time he was very quiet. He usually had his sketch book with him and would sometimes sit near the sales desk and draw for a little while. The morning I told Roger I was leaving, the young man was in the store early and no one else was around. I was so uncharacteristically quiet that I felt the need to explain the reason for my silence. I also needed to share my pain, so I told him that I had broken the news to my husband that morning about leaving him. The young man never said a word. He looked into my eyes and, acknowledging my anguish with a nod, he sat down and started to draw. For the next two or three hours he sat beside me and sketched abstract designs. Other customers came and went, but he stayed right there. In his own way, I knew he was giving me support. He was like an anchor that day, keeping me from falling into an abyss. I was enormously grateful.

## Living the Lie

So, Roger wanted to take action, but I didn't want to tell anyone. I knew it might be a long while until I found the financial means and emotional courage to actually make the move. I saw no good reason to upset the whole family prematurely. For a while, he became very quiet and withdrawn. Our son would ask me, "What's wrong with Dad?" I couldn't answer for Roger, so I would say I didn't know and suggest that we just give him a lot of space to work things out.

I thought my heart was in the right place by being secretive. I desperately wanted to protect my children from knowing anything until I was sure of when and how I was going to make the move. Our other son lived across the country on the Air Force base in New Mexico with his wife. It was easier to keep the news from them because they weren't privy to the daily happenings in our home. Since I wasn't ready to inform my children, I didn't want to discuss it with anyone that knew our family, lest they slip and my children hear the news second hand.

All of this deception took a heavy toll on me and my husband. He wasn't in total agreement with me but, to his credit, he abided by my rules for a very, *very* long time. It was another two years before we even *told* our sons. In the meantime, I struggled to maintain a facade with my extended family and our mutual friends that everything was fine when I really felt like I was dying inside.

I don't know that telling our children earlier would have served them better. Even if it would have, I did what I thought was best and what I believed I needed to do to survive. I have come to believe that everything happens for a reason and that reason is our spiritual growth. We each attract situations into our life that will provide the lessons we need to continue to evolve spiritually. So I believe that everything happened exactly the way it needed to happen for every one, in spite of how any of us might have wished it had happened differently.

Since I remained in our home for so long after telling Roger that I wanted to leave, we eventually fell back into a familiar routine, but thoughts of my leaving often punctuated the silence. To add to the stress, Roger made the decision to leave his job. He had been working in an unbelievably stressful environment and I fully supported him in his decision. We expected that he would find another job quickly but that didn't happen. Soon after he quit, I found out that the art supply store where I was employed would soon be closing. I think Roger thought I would run right out and find another job, but I was determined to make a go of it by selling my artwork from home. When he finally asked me when I was going to go to work I said, "I *am* working!"

Four months later, with our bank account almost depleted, he found another position. Perhaps I was being selfish and irresponsible, but with my ever more spiritual outlook, I was beginning to take risks based on a belief in myself and a benevolent higher power. To Roger's credit, he had supported me when I decided to leave nursing. He supported me my whole adult life in most anything I wanted to do, but he didn't seem to share my new beliefs. For reasons I couldn't grasp at the time, I wasn't able to find the words to explain them to him. It became more and more difficult to stay with him and still live life the way I wanted and needed to.

**Visions**

Although I knew it was very important for me to experience being on my own, I was beginning to experience mental pictures of me walking hand in hand with another man. We were of equal stature physically and seemed to be walking forward through life together as lovers and best friends. These weren't so much imaginings as they were like snapshots of the future flashing in my brain. That had happened once before in my life and what I had pictured had occurred, exactly as I had seen it. So I was beginning to think that

I would eventually be in another relationship. However, it was extremely important to me that Roger understood and believed that I was not leaving him for someone else. I was leaving for myself. My primary goal was to get to know and fall in love with the part of me that could be completely happy *on my own.*

There was a tremendous amount of love between Roger and me, but I knew that, on my part at least, there was a small element of neediness as well; a sense of dependence and not feeling complete without a partner. So even though I could imagine myself eventually *desiring* to be with someone else, I knew that *needing* them would not make for a healthy relationship. I remembered counseling our oldest son when he got married that needing someone is not the same as loving a person. Now it was time for me to explore that advice on a deeper level.

# 2000—Exploring

## Staying Open

By now, I was practically inhaling literature that had to do with spirituality. I wasn't searching for a religious doctrine to follow. I wanted to learn more about looking within myself for answers. As I opened up to new ways of viewing life, I began to see a bigger picture; to believe in a universal force much greater than myself. My experiences were beginning to validate some of my beliefs in small, synchronistic ways. Ever since that night, almost four years earlier, when I feebly asked for help, guidance seemed to be coming to me in small, digestible bites: an article here, an overheard conversation there, a comment from a stranger in the grocery line, something I would hear on the radio.

At first, I saw all these things as coincidence, but the evidence was mounting. I had reached the point where I could no longer deny that something profound was happening. I was finally becoming aware of this synchronicity and began using it to guide me on my journey of self-discovery. The more aware I became, the more it seemed to occur.

A funny example happened one day while driving my car. I was going over and over in my mind whether or not to leave my marriage. Should I? Shouldn't I? Should I? Shouldn't I? I was so confused and overwhelmed that I thought my brain was going to implode. To get my mind off my troubles, I turned on the radio. The first song I heard repeated the same lyrics throughout the entire song. It kept telling me that "the change will do you good." I burst out laughing, which was great comic relief, but I also began daring to dream that someday I really would be on my own. It was still very scary to me and I needed a way to try it on for size.

I began with an off-season weekend away in Rockport, Massachusetts. Some of my friends were shocked that I would go on a vacation without my family. I can't actually remember what I told my husband. I probably said I needed an artist's retreat. I did think that I would do a lot of painting, but instead, I found myself doing a lot of nothing. I walked or sat by the ocean for hours. One night I took my lawn chair across the street and sat by the water all by myself at midnight. The moonlight playing off the water was gorgeous. I relaxed and focused on the beauty before me. I was so exhausted from trying to figure out what to do with my life that my mind was taking a much needed rest.

## Maryland

Another opportunity to be alone came along later that year. I was asked to house and pet sit for my brother's family in Maryland for a week. I jumped at the chance, figuring it was the closest thing to experiencing being on my own that I would get at that time. My mom thought that I would get bored and lonely and be sorry that I went. Mom was wrong. Not only was I not bored, I didn't even *want* to call home.

I'll admit, the first morning there I did feel a bit shaky as I sat in that relatively unfamiliar house far from my home. Driving a car with a manual stick shift for the first time in years on unfamiliar roads and caring for two enormous dogs who could have easily taken *me* for a ride were part of the challenge. I used their long driveway and quiet side street to begin getting used to the standard transmission in the car. I was surprised to see how easily it all came back to me. My greatest fear was getting lost. Each day I ventured a little farther from home until I got used to the area. My confidence boosted, I began enjoying my independence.

The first night when I stated out loud that it was time to go to bed, their beautiful Samoyed dogs took their cue and bounded up the stairs ahead of me. When I got upstairs, I was surprised to see the dogs already on the queen size waterbed, the old kind with no baffles to subdue the waves. They were romping about joyously and inviting me with their characteristic Samoyed grin to join them. They were quite confused and dismayed when I made them get down. They would stay on the floor a while but, just as I was falling asleep, they would leap onto the bed again, causing waves that would nearly catapult me to the floor. It took most of the week before I finally had an uninterrupted night's sleep.

Two days later, when the gardener left the gate open, the dogs got loose. My heart was pounding as I ran into the house to grab their leashes and treats to lure them back. I could hear the answering machine relaying a message from my sister-in-law in the background. In a cheery vacation voice she was saying, "Hi Paula, this is Penny. I'm just calling to see how everything is going." *Not very well!* I thought as I ignored the phone and raced out the door. Being similar to sled dogs, I feared that my brother's beloved pets would just keep on running and I'd never get them back. As it turned out, they returned rather quickly of their own accord and it didn't take too much coaxing to get them back into the house, safe and sound. Fortunately, the young woman who would be taking over the house sitting for week two was a pet groomer, so the dogs were white, fluffy and free of burrs when my brother's family returned.

As the week went on, I began to relax into my new surroundings and enjoy myself. Before leaving for vacation, my brother handed me a CD he thought I would find interesting. I had brought my art supplies with me and, feeling a lot more settled in by midweek, I decided to listen to the CD one night while painting. The music was primal with chants and tribal drum rhythms. I had never heard anything quite like it before. I often painted to music, but this was different. With no one around except the dogs, I soon lost my inhibition and found myself dancing to the evocative sounds with wild abandon. I danced to the point of exhaustion and then slipped into a deep meditation. When I returned to painting, my work took on a whole different feeling. Inspiration seemed to come from a deeper place inside of me than I had ever tapped before. The music was no longer just a backdrop. It became an integral part of my work. My brushstrokes began to synchronize with the beat of the drums. After that night, I often found myself regularly dancing to music while I painted. That particular CD remained the most compelling of them all.

Being away for those six days was very telling. I not only met my challenges, I thoroughly enjoyed my freedom. I loved being on my own.

# 2001—Ready, Set . . .

### Getting Clearer

By the spring of 2001, *on my own* had become my mantra. A pivotal moment came one morning when I was alone in our house except for our two pets. I had just settled into my meditation when our dog indicated that he needed to be let outside. It was a simple request and it was only the dog but, once again, I was being pulled away from the quiet, uninterrupted solitude I so desperately wanted.

Through meditation, I was discovering another world; a place where all was peaceful, loving and safe; where the busy activities of life didn't seem so important. I could retreat from the world of people and things and go deep inside myself. It wasn't so much an escape, as it was a way of centering myself so that I could then function better in the world. By focusing on my breath, progressively relaxing each part of my body, and getting very still, I could gradually stop my mind from chattering and begin to listen. I wasn't sure exactly what I expected to hear. I just knew that I was always much calmer and had a healthier outlook on life after meditating. Having to get up and let the dog out was the final straw. I found myself standing in the middle of my kitchen, clenching my hair in my fists and screaming at the top of my lungs, "I JUST WANT TO BE ALONE!"

## A New Job

I knew what I wanted to do and I needed to find a way to do it. Selling a painting every now and then wasn't going to give me the financial freedom I needed, so I decided to look for a job. The very next day, I started my morning by meditating and asking for guidance on where to begin my search. Through books I was reading, I was learning that I could ask for guidance with a particular issue and then relax and see what thoughts came up during or after meditation. I was hoping to get an art-related job. In my mind, I had been mapping out which galleries I would approach, but I received much different guidance. During my meditation, the thought came to me that I should go to a nearby shopping mall. At first, I couldn't imagine how I would find an art-related job there. Then I remembered a kiosk in the mall that had some artwork I liked, so I went to check it out. I discovered that it had closed, so I decided to walk around the mall while thinking where to go next. To my surprise, I came across an art gallery that had just opened. I walked in and took a look around. When a sales woman asked if I had any questions, I was startled to hear myself say, "Yes, do you have any job openings?"

"Why, yes!" she replied, quite surprised. "We just had an employee quit last night."

The next thing I knew she was on the phone to the owner. Half an hour later, I found myself in the middle of a job interview.

I instantly fell in love with the gallery owner. She was warm, enthusiastic and genuine. Her smile lit up the room and she had the most heavenly laugh I had ever heard. Later I learned that her family owned a parrot that mimicked their laughter. *How appropriate*, I thought. She offered the job to me so quickly that I ended up telling her I needed time to decide. I was proud of myself for feeling secure enough to take the time I felt I needed. The following morning I called the owner back and accepted her offer on the condition that I could have time off to go on a family vacation that had already been planned. It was agreed. The job was delightful in many ways. It also became an enormous classroom for my personal growth.

**New Mexico**

The vacation planned was a trip to New Mexico to visit our oldest son, Michael, and our daughter-in-law, Leslie. They were stationed on the Air Force base in

Albuquerque. We had only been there one other time and we were quite excited to go back. One of the highlights of our trip was a visit to the Acoma Indian Reservation, also called Sky City. It is one of the oldest pueblos in America. The buildings sit atop a mesa situated seemingly in the middle of nowhere. There are no modern utilities. It was so quiet, secluded and peaceful at the top of that high plateau that a deep feeling of hushed reverence swept over me. I felt like I was on sacred ground and I should tread softly and talk in whispers. Standing at the edge of those steep cliffs, looking out from that ancient place was a very powerful experience.

Midweek, we planned to go into Santa Fe. I was excited to be visiting such an art mecca, but I was a little concerned that my family might be bored touring shops and galleries. The way I recall it is that everyone *agreed* that they wanted to go into the city; however, the closer we got to our destination, the less interested everyone else seemed to be. I began to feel responsible for making sure that everyone was happy and Roger, in particular, wanted "a plan."

"Where are we going?" he'd say.

"I don't know. I've never been to Santa Fe before. I just want to find some art galleries to explore."

"Which ones? Do you have any names?" he'd push.

"No, not really. There are streets lined with galleries. I'm sure we'll find some nice ones," I reassured him.

"Do you know which streets? Do you know how much further we have to go?" he asked.

On and on it went. He wanted a plan. I did not have one. I was feeling pressured, unable to follow my own guidance. I finally said, "OK, I promise we will stop at the first gallery that we come across."

From the minute we walked in the door, it didn't feel right. In fact, it felt downright creepy! I wanted to run out of the building, but I had promised to stop there. The 'art' we saw in that building was disturbing. Everything seemed to have been created for shock value. In one room there was a continuous video recording of a voluptuous woman starting to unbutton her blouse. Each time she got down to loosening a button that would reveal her breasts, a gunshot sounded. The same scene played over and over. I was becoming more disgusted by the minute and soon declared, "I have had enough!" Fortunately, the rest of my family agreed. We rarely brought up that part of our trip because it was so disturbing. However, I was grateful for the experience. It was a tremendous lesson about what happens when I stop listening to and following my own guidance in order to make someone else happy.

We visited a few other galleries that were much nicer and I began to relax, but I felt that the others didn't. Only having one afternoon to explore a place that I easily could have explored for months, I finally made a decision that I think surprised us all. I told them that I was venturing off on my own and that I would meet them back at a certain place in about two hours. As I walked away I was shaking because I had been bold enough to step out on my own and do what I wanted to do.

For the next two hours I let my instincts guide me. I found many wonderful galleries to visit and people to talk with, but it was the last conversation I had that afternoon that proved to be the most crucial. When I met with my family back at our designated spot, I asked if they would wait while I went into just one more gallery. The owner struck up a conversation with me. He told me that he, too, had left his job to pursue his art. He said he wasn't making as much money, but that he was very, very happy. He said that his family didn't really understand him, but that was okay. He had to do what he did. Then he pointed outside to where my own family stood. In broken English he said, "Look at them. They no understand you. They no want wait for you. You can't make them understand. What your heart tell you? That what you do." With tears welling up, I took his hand. "Thank you," I said. "You have no idea how much you have helped me. I have a very big decision to make tonight."

"I know, I *know*!" he said. "That's why I tell you . . . it's why I talk to you."

His words touched me so deeply because we had primarily come to New Mexico for me to tell my oldest son and his wife, in person, that I planned to separate from Roger. Because I saw myself as the bad guy, it never even occurred to me that he and I could tell them together. I felt singularly responsible for everyone's pain and that, therefore, I was the one who had to deliver the bad news. My anxiety over doing that was so great that just thinking about it would nearly make my knees buckle. The same question was still always foremost in my mind. *How can I be true to myself, to what my heart was calling me to do, and not cause unbearable pain to my loved ones?* The thought of telling them was so overwhelming to me that I was considering backing out of the conversation and, quite possibly, out of my plan to leave the marriage. It was the conversation with the gallery owner in Santa Fe that gave me the courage to move forward.

That evening, I broke the news to our oldest son and his wife. For reasons that I can no longer fathom, I insisted that we not tell our youngest son, age 16, yet. I guess I felt it was best to wait until I knew when and how I would be able to move out before telling him. I was so afraid of his reaction, but later, when I finally told him, he seemed to handle the news more calmly than anyone else in our immediate family. But, on this occasion, I asked my husband to take him for a walk while I sat in the living room and spoke to our other son and his wife. Somehow I made it through the conversation. Because they lived so far away from us, I think it was easy for them to have missed the telltale signs, so the news came as a complete surprise. It was when my husband returned and, in a private moment, I saw my usually undemonstrative oldest son lean heavily into his dad's arms that my heart completely broke. To complicate matters further, I had put him and his wife in the position of having to hide the news and their raw feelings from our youngest son. What the hell was I thinking?!

My only consolation was that I was doing the best I knew how to do at that time. How I wish that my husband and I had sat our two sons and daughter-in-law down and told them together as a family. The pain and anger would still have been felt, but it most likely would have been easier for everyone to deal with it together. I believed in my heart that I was coming from a place of love, but I was really operating out of fear. I created a situation that only generated more fear, secrecy and doubt. I can't go back and relive that time in my life, nor would I want to, but I can view it now from a different perspective. I accept in my heart that everything had to happen exactly the way it did for everyone involved, even if the reasons were not always clear to me.

**Preparing to Leap**

Life, as I knew it, was unraveling. I had set the wheels in motion and I knew there was no turning back. As my old life was coming apart, I was privately building a new one to take its place. I began having dreams about vast, physical carnage and destruction, about buildings and cities crumbling all around me. In the ruins, I always found a kitten that had survived unscathed. I believed the kitten symbolized me in my new life. I also dreamed that our family car was partially buried in an avalanche with me, Roger, and our youngest son inside. In the dream, only my son and I survived. I wondered if that foretold that I wouldn't stay in contact with my husband after the separation, although that wasn't what I wanted. I didn't know at the time that the dream meant so much more.

I also had a dream about my health that got my attention. I dreamed that I was hanging from a large wooden beam, trying to 'walk it' with my hands. I was struggling to hold on. A genderless Being reached down and took my hand. As it did, there was a feeling of incredible warmth and a sense of our hands merging together. The Being lifted me up so I could stand on the beam and walk across it effortlessly. "See how easy it is? There's no need to struggle," He/She said. I was led to a lounge chair to lie down. I felt a deep peace and relaxation wash over me that was like nothing I had ever experienced before. I wanted it to never end. The Being stood near the left side of my head. He/She looked at me and gently said, "There's a small cancer there." Then I woke up.

I didn't feel alarmed, but I immediately scheduled my overdue, annual physical and had all the usual tests done. Nothing showed up, so I decided to return to my skin doctor who had removed a basal cell growth from my left cheek a few years ago. Sure enough, although it was still small, he said the growth had recurred and needed to be removed. It was on the left side of my face, right where the Being had been standing in my dream.

In spite of that little scare, I kept building my new life, which included creating a whole new circle of friends; people with whom it felt safe to share my hopes and dreams; people who understood and viewed life from what I considered a more spiritual perspective and who lent me guidance and support along the way. At home, I found myself spending more and more time alone in my art studio. One day, my husband stood at the door and said, "Do you realize that, other than for eating and sleeping, you have completely moved into this room?" I was also gradually collecting any decorative items from the house that I knew I would be taking with me and replacing them with my husband's things so that there wouldn't be a shocking, physical emptiness when I finally moved out. I couldn't prevent the emotional emptiness, but I hoped I could at least soften the blow.

As I said, the process of moving out took much longer than I had anticipated. In hindsight, I was shocked and very much ashamed when I realized that three years had passed between the telling and the doing. How could so much time have elapsed? My lack of finances was a huge factor, but I believe there were other subtle forces at work as well. Although my husband was saying he was anxious to have me leave so he could "stop waiting for the other shoe to drop," he was also making it increasingly inviting for me to stay. He picked up where I had slacked off in making our house cozy and inviting with fires in the fireplace and hot meals ready when I got home from work. He was also extra kind and attentive. Although he never said it, I imagined he was hoping that I would change my mind and stay. All in all, Roger made it easy for me to coast for quite some time. But this also added to my sense of guilt.

One day I received a call from someone who berated me for how I was conducting my life: for how hurtful, selfish and uncaring I was; for taking too long to move out on my own; and many other things. This unexpected attack left me reeling. How dare anyone judge me that way! After the call, I cried. I screamed. I cursed. I threw pillows. I nearly kicked the stuffing out of my living room chair. Then I went outside for a very brisk walk in the dark until there wasn't an ounce of fight left in me. It is only in looking back that I can see how I attracted this verbal assault because of my own guilt. The caller mirrored back to me everything that I feared was true. Had I been selfish and uncaring? Did I have poor timing? Had I made poor decisions that needlessly hurt a lot of people? The one I was really kicking the stuffing out of was me. And it hurt . . . it hurt a lot.

Once I understood how I had helped create that situation, it became easier to begin the process of forgiving the caller. I discovered that each time I was able to forgive someone else for a perceived wrong, I was really forgiving that behavior in myself. I knew that ultimately forgiveness was the only thing that could set me free.

And how I longed to be free! I was so tired of being misunderstood. I imagined that everyone in my family thought I lived a fairy tale and that I had created this spiritual dream world that gave me a false sense of security. Conversely, I believed that they had no sense of the place of strength I was coming from. I thought *they* were the ones living a fantasy by thinking that they were smart enough to control their own lives without believing in a higher power. I wanted to help them see the light. I kept thinking it was my job to save them. How arrogant of me! I can see now that, by feeling spiritually *superior*, I was doing exactly the same thing that I was accusing them of.

I also felt tremendous pressure from my family to return to nursing in order to secure the finances I needed to move out on my own. But, there are some things you know deep in your soul and I knew I could not go back. There were too many emotional wounds from that part of my life that hadn't healed yet. I also *knew* there was something else I was meant to do with my life; something that was more rewarding and uplifting for me. I didn't know what it was yet, but I knew with every fiber of my being that I needed to create a space for whatever *it* was. I was finally starting to believe in myself, so I dug my heels in deep.

# 2002—GO!

**Moving Out**

Spring is a time of change and new growth. That was certainly true in my own life. In March of 2002, almost three years after first voicing my need to be on my own, and after many months of searching, I finally found an affordable apartment that felt warm, welcoming and safe to me. It was advertised as having "spacious, sunny rooms" and it lived up to that description. Besides the sunshine, the first thing I noticed was that the apartment had all new windows and kitchen cabinets with drawers that worked perfectly. Having looked at many older buildings, I was aware of the problems inherent in dealing with windows and drawers that didn't work well. As a carpenter, my dad had always made sure that everything in our home was kept in good working order. As I went around testing the windows and drawers, I suddenly recalled the desk my dad had built for me when I was a teenager that I still use today. I always loved its beautifully crafted drawers that slid easily on gliders. With that thought, I *knew* my dad was giving me his seal of approval. His presence felt so real that it was all I could do not to start giggling.

Before making a commitment, I wanted to go back and view the apartment at night to see if it still felt safe and welcoming. All the lights were on when I arrived. Stepping through the front door into that warm and cheerful space felt magical to me. I had been saying for a long time that I would know when I had found the right place, but I didn't understand exactly how. That night I had my answer. I was still very nervous about moving, but for the first time, my excitement outweighed my fear.

Both my husband and Greg came with me to view the apartment that night. The first thing Roger noted was that it felt "just like Mt. Washington Street" where we lived when we first got married. I had not seen the connection, but he was absolutely right. No wonder it felt familiar! He watched as I went from room to room, measuring to see if my new life would fit into that space. Later he commented that he knew I would take the apartment. When I asked how, he said, "Even though you were nervous, I could feel your excitement."

A few days later, I met with the landlady to pick up the key and sign the lease. My hands were shaking so hard I could barely write my name. She was very kind and supportive. "I'm sure you'll be just fine," she said. I didn't even know this woman, but I think I would have listened to kind words from *anyone* at that moment. I had gone there straight from work and decided to celebrate by stopping on the way to pick up a pizza to enjoy in my new home. I even brought a small cushion to sit on. Once I was alone, I walked from room to room, marveling that the space was all mine. It was like having a blank canvas on which to paint my new life. I could hardly wait to begin.

**On My Own**

Over the next few days, I began transferring my smaller belongings into the apartment. I didn't have a lot of furniture, just two living room chairs from my mom's house and a bedroom set from my aunt. My mattress and kitchen table were to be delivered from the stores where I bought them. My cousin had also given me a living room lamp and curtains. I was given almost all the major things I needed in order to set up housekeeping for free and right on time. It was as if the universe was supporting me in my decision. This pattern would repeat itself again and again over the next few years. Once I became clear about what I intended to do and started taking action, everything that I needed to succeed would begin to appear from *out of the blue.*

I tried to take as few things from our home as possible. I very much wanted to make a fresh start, but more importantly, I didn't want to leave a physical hole. I was doing everything in my power to make the transition as gentle as possible. It never even occurred to me to ask Roger to move out of the house because *I* was the one who so desperately wanted change. I believe Roger loved me unconditionally. He wanted me to be happy. Although the pain was evident in his eyes, his sad smiles and his long, withdrawn silences, he loved me enough to graciously let me go. He not only came to view the apartment with me, he drove the U-Haul truck to pick up my furniture and, together, he and Greg moved everything for me. From my perspective, he was helping me move in. I imagine that, from his perspective, he was helping me to move out.

My bed wasn't delivered until the next day, so I spent one more night at our house. In the morning I went to work knowing that I would be sleeping in my new place for the first time that night. All day my thoughts bounced equally between excitement and fear. My co-worker didn't say too much about my moving that day, but she returned from her break with a homey, cinnamon apple scented candle sitting in a saucer. All she said as she handed it to me was, "I knew that tonight was weighing on you." The first thing I did when I got inside the apartment was light the candle. I carried it with me from room to room that night, wondering if I would ever be able to feel like I was 'home' again.

Gradually, I became more at peace in my new space. I delighted in decorating each room. It was more than just experimenting with color and design. It was very important that my surroundings reflected the person I was becoming. Piece by piece, I was putting together a new home, a new life and a new me.

Right after I moved, I sent a letter to our relatives and friends to inform them of my move and how to reach each of us. I tried to explain my reasons for leaving and reassure people that Roger and I were still friends and that we were both comfortable being invited to the same functions. It surprised me that hardly anyone even mentioned the letter. I thought it would help make them more comfortable about approaching us, but I never knew if it did or not. I realized I may have used the letter in an attempt to defend myself, as if I owed the whole world an explanation for why I wanted to live life on my own terms.

Actually, it would be another nine years before *I* completely understood, and admitted to myself, the real reason I needed to be on my own.

## Time for Introspection

Our youngest son remained living with Roger. I had originally looked for a two bedroom apartment so he could stay with me as often as he liked. He assured me that it wasn't necessary. He would be getting his driver's license soon and said he could visit me whenever he wanted. I had agonized over telling him about my leaving for over two years, so I was relieved to see him dealing with my move in what seemed to be a healthy way. After I moved, I still saw him regularly. I saw Roger and my close friends from time to time, but mostly I was glad to be alone and retreat from the world. I felt I could not learn any more about myself and who I wanted to become from the outside world. It was time to go within. I spent more and more time reading, painting, and meditating. My only television was a 30-year-old black and white with only three channels and horrible reception. I almost never used it except to occasionally *listen to* Oprah.

I used the largest room of my apartment for my art studio and the smaller, adjacent room as my living room. Developing my art career was very important to me. As I became bolder and took more risks, my artwork had become bolder as well. After moving to the apartment, I found myself using huge brushes and house painting rollers to create large, abstract pieces. I dreamed of being a self-supporting artist. More than a dream, I needed to prove to myself, and everyone else, that I could succeed. I had spent the last few years preaching to people that they could be happy and successful by following their dreams. Now it was time for me to live up to those words.

# 2003—Getting in the Boat

### Taking a Stand

It was also time to deal with my inability to stand up for myself, which I had never fully dealt with during my nursing career. As I alluded to earlier, my gallery job would prove to be very fertile ground for personal growth. The players were different, but the issue was still the same. How much crap was I going to take before I learned to say, "Enough!" As it turned out, I would take quite a lot.

We worked on commission at the gallery. Most of my competition came from one particular salesperson. He was very difficult to read. He would be kind to my face while, at the same time, lying, cheating and stealing from me every chance he got. He was so smooth that I would often wonder *did he really just do what I think he did?* Instead of confronting him, I would chicken out or begin to second-guess myself. I got so frustrated that I would be punching the roof of the car with my fists on my ride home.

I did eventually learn to stand up to him. I'm pleased to say I managed to do it in a kind, loving manner that allowed both of us to maintain our dignity. I sat down with him one day, after discovering he had cheated me out of a very big sale. I told him there were many things I liked about him, but that I did not like how he was behaving; that I could not trust him and I would no longer tolerate his behavior. I then proceeded to tell him that I was going to claim the commission from that particular sale for myself. He was so stunned that, with each word I said, he backed his chair up further until he had backed himself against the wall. That did not stop him from trying to sabotage the sale again a few days later, but the important thing was that I had finally stood up for myself.

I understand now that this man was one of my greatest teachers. One day, years later, as I sat contemplating why he triggered such anger in me, I came to a realization. Every time he cheated me, he put me in a position where I knew I should stand up to him. I hated confrontations and he exposed that weakness in me. It was really myself I was angry at for not having the courage to take a stand.

**Live Performance**

What *did* give me courage, and made my life richer, was my ever-increasing awareness that my dad was always with me in spirit. A few months earlier, I had heard a song by Paul Simon (my father's name was also Paul) about a father loving his daughter. I was hoping to hear it again to catch more of the lyrics. I spent one whole afternoon trying to find the song on my car radio to no avail.

Later that evening, as I was reading a book, the thought popped into my head to turn on the television. As previously mentioned, that wasn't something I did very often. Even though I was enjoying my book, the thought persisted. I finally gave in. I didn't know what I was looking for. When I turned it on, an awards show was playing. I knew that in between the award presentations they would have musical entertainment, so I decided to stay on that channel for a while. A minute later, who came on stage to perform but Paul Simon! There he was, right in front of me, singing these words:

"I'm gonna watch you shine
Gonna watch you grow
Gonna paint a sign
So you'll always know
As long as one and one is two
There could never be a father
Who loved his daughter more than I love you"

## Mother Mary

Someone else was watching over me as well, but I was unaware of it. What I thought was just a chance encounter with a customer at the gallery called it to my attention. Somehow our conversation came around to the subject of the Blessed Mother. The man told me that he used to have handfuls of medals that were blessed at a place called Medjugorje. The Blessed Mother has been said to have appeared there many times. It didn't occur to me to question how the blessings came about. I was listening to his many stories of miraculous healings that had come to recipients of those medals. "I might still have one," he said. "I'll bring it to you."

Although I had been raised Catholic, the Virgin Mary had never been a prominent figure to me. In fact, thoughts of her really never entered my mind. I could not understand why he was offering the medal to me. I also did not think there were any problems in my life big enough to warrant receiving the medal. I told him that I would hold onto it until I met someone who needed it. A few months passed and I had forgotten about his promise, so I was surprised when he showed up and handed me a medal. I thanked him again saying, "I'm not sure yet who this is for, but I will be sure to give it to someone who really needs it." Wrapping his hands around mine, he looked deep into my eyes and smiled. "It's for you," he said gently. "It's for you." It would be another two years before I believed him.

## Gone Dancing

I also felt my dad watching over me when I went to my first singles dance. All my life I had wanted to dance. Although my husband tried, he was never very comfortable on the dance floor. I always believed that if I could dance with someone who knew how to lead, I would easily be able to follow. I was finally able to test that theory out when Roger and I attended a friend's wedding together. When my friend's brother asked me to dance, I discovered that, under his expert guidance, I could follow him with ease. We danced two delightful dances. When I returned to my table, I tried not to let my happiness show because I didn't want to make Roger feel bad, but I was breathless with excitement.

That experience encouraged me to think about going to singles dances. I was not looking for a romantic partner. I simply wanted someone to dance with. One night, when I got tired of waiting for friends to go with me, I decided to go to a dance by myself. This was a huge step for me. I used to go lots of places on my own, but dancing was different. I didn't know what to expect.

I sat in the parking lot for about twenty minutes, watching people go into the building. I wanted to make sure I was dressed appropriately and that the crowd was around my age. When I stepped into the hall, it was fairly dark. As my eyes adjusted, I could see that there were round tables set up on three sides of the dance floor and a DJ along the forth. There were extra chairs lining two walls. I walked over and sat in one of them next to another woman who was sitting alone. I tried to strike up a conversation with her, but she seemed rather grouchy. I was so nervous that I wanted to run out the door. Just then a kind looking, older gentleman came over and asked me to dance. I smiled to myself when I learned his name was Paul. He was very friendly and went out of his way to introduce me to some of his friends. One of them had eyes that looked so much like my father's that it was startling. I had to keep looking away because the similarity was so unnerving. But with the two reminders of my dad within the first ten minutes of being there, I felt it was a sign telling me it was safe to stay. I am so glad I did. I didn't sit down for the rest of the evening. I returned home exhausted, smiling from ear to ear.

I have never been a fan of bumper stickers, but if I'd had to choose one, it would have said *I'd rather be dancing!* I went every weekend. I would arrive when the doors opened at 7pm and stay until the hall closed at midnight. For those five hours, I was in heaven. The more I danced, the better I got at it. The better I got, the more I wanted to dance. I met many wonderful people and gradually acclimated myself to the nighttime social scene. I always thought I had good people skills, but it took me a while to learn how to graciously turn down unwanted partners, choose between two simultaneous requests, or extricate myself from those who wanted to monopolize my time. Overall though, the dance hall provided a safe atmosphere. Most everyone was truly there to just dance, meet friends and have fun.

For me dancing was, and still is, an incredibly joyful form of self expression. It is such an integral part of me that I have trouble understanding how someone can *not* be able to move to the beat of music. When I made a mental list of the characteristics I wanted in a romantic partner, being able to dance was close to the top of my list.

**Finding My Voice**

I made another bold decision when I joined Toastmasters International public speaking organization. For years, whenever I listened to a speaker at an event, I would always envision myself being the one standing up there with the microphone. Joining Toastmasters was a way to test out and improve my speaking skills. I made many friends there. Great business contacts and opportunities also came my way. I had not anticipated that the group would also become a forum for the motivational work I longed to do. Not every speech I gave was of that genre, but many were. With such a diverse audience, I wasn't always sure how my words were being received, but I gradually began getting positive feedback, not only on my speaking ability, but on the content of my speeches as well. I even received a note from someone who I didn't think was that interested in my messages saying, "You have managed to teach me more than you would know."

## Get In the Boat

One of my favorite things to speak about was following inner guidance. I definitely had to do that one afternoon while sitting by the river near my home. As I sat on the stone wall, a man who looked to be about my age cruised by in his motorboat. He was alone. For some inexplicable reason, I had the feeling he was going to speak to me. So, I wasn't too surprised when he waved as he passed by. On his way back up the river, he slowed his boat and said, "Hello." We struck up a light conversation that quickly turned into a deeper discussion about living on one's own. It was a natural progression and I felt very comfortable talking to him. However, it was difficult for him to hold his boat steady off shore and there was too much physical distance between us to talk easily. The next thing I knew he was shaking his head in disbelief and saying, "This isn't something I would normally do, but I feel compelled to invite you aboard so we can continue this conversation." And even more surprisingly, I found myself saying, "Yes."

I couldn't believe my own ears. Getting in a boat with a complete stranger? No one knew I was at the river. They wouldn't even know where to look for me if I disappeared! But underlying all those thoughts was a growing certainty that we were supposed to talk and that everything would be okay. We cruised the river for about an hour. The man was considering leaving his wife and was nervous about being on his own. He had many questions and seemed to find information about my own experience helpful. We had a deep and very rewarding conversation. No contact information was exchanged. We both seemed to know that this was a onetime encounter.

I was quite pleased with myself that day. I was pleased that I was learning how to listen to and trust my inner guidance. I took all my precautionary thoughts into account, but then I went deeper to make my decision. My heart told me it was okay and I was right. I'm glad I listened. When I shared my adventure with a circle of my newest friends, I had to laugh at their reactions. I knew my friend, Mary, would understand my decision. As I told my tale, she sat there smiling and nodding in agreement, but the others were appalled. "Oh my God, Paula! How could you? You could have been killed! Nobody knew where you were!" On and on they went. I tried my best to explain, but they could not seem to understand why sometimes . . . you have to get in the boat.

# 2004—Spiritual/Midlife crisis

**Popovers**

I followed my inner guidance the following year when I sought out a particular person to give me a psychic reading. I was glad I did because something she said during the reading helped me to understand the reason for a difficult experience I had endured long ago. It clearly demonstrated to me that there is a reason for everything, but sometimes we do not understand the reason because we simply cannot stand back far enough to see the bigger picture.

I was home from college for the weekend and my new boyfriend was joining our family for Sunday dinner. I don't recall anything my mother cooked that day except popovers. They are a type of roll that you cook in a muffin tin and they are supposed to rise up high and be light and fluffy. These were not. Being a notoriously good cook, but her own worst critic, Mom wasn't happy with the results. But, this time, she wasn't the one criticizing.

My dad had mistakenly had too much to drink, which was *totally*, TOTALLY, out of character for him. He began critiquing Mom's popovers. "Kind of heavy, don't you think? Could probably use these to jack up the car with." On and on he went. I was shocked and extremely embarrassed when he began juggling the popovers and proceeded to throw them out the open kitchen window. My mom hid her irritation pretty well, but I burst into tears and ran from the table mortified. My boyfriend followed me into the other room. At that point, my dad realized he had crossed the line and apologized. We were soon peacefully settled back around the table, but because this behavior was so unusual for him, it was a very traumatic experience for me.

Now, here I was, thirty-four years later, having a psychic reading. The reader started to share some information that she said was coming from my dad who had passed on fourteen years earlier. I very much wanted to believe I was hearing messages from him, but I was still a bit skeptical. Then, out of the blue, the reader said, "I'm seeing muffin tins.....some kind of rolls maybe?" I jumped out of my chair and screamed, "POPOVERS!" I hadn't been thinking about that long ago event, so I knew she wasn't reading my mind. It certainly wasn't something I talked about and, even if I had, this woman didn't know me. So, how could she have known unless my dad sent her that vision? To me, that was proof positive that he was there, watching over me and guiding me. I was sure of it . . . and all because of popovers.

## Lost

For the past few years I had been cultivating what I called more *spiritual* beliefs. I had strayed from my Catholic upbringing when I was in college and hadn't given religion much thought since then. I was quite happy with my new belief that we each needed to find the truth from our own deep place of inner knowing. I believed it was more a sense of remembering something we already knew. I also believed that this remembering would ultimately guide us to the universal truth that love is the only thing that is *real*; that this truth doesn't differ from person to person, place to place or culture to culture; that it is true for everyone. To me, spirituality had nothing to do with formal religion or an external set of guidelines. I found that when I let love, not fear, guide all my decisions, I didn't need anyone to tell me how to live my life.

That was until a new co-worker entered my life. I instantly liked her and we became friends, but she was extremely religious and my constant contact with her began to erode my confidence in my own beliefs. Her strong faith reminded me very much of my Catholic upbringing and I began to question whether or not I was truly headed in the right direction. My mind waged a constant battle between old beliefs (or should I say fears) that the church had ingrained in me as a child and the new beliefs I had come to on my own. I was so confused that I thought my brain would explode. I found it difficult to focus on making any other decisions in my life, even tiny everyday ones, until I had come to terms with this big one. I needed a foundation on which to base my life's decisions and the one I had built was in danger of crumbling.

Life has a funny way of mirroring whatever is happening inside of us. During this confusing time, I went to visit a friend of mine. I had been to her new house once before and was certain I knew which exit to take off the highway, so I didn't bring the directions. I ended up way off course in the middle of a big city that I was unfamiliar with. When I stopped to call my friend for help, I realized I didn't have her new number with me because it was on the sheet of directions. Her new name and address weren't in the phone book yet, so there was no way to contact her. All I could do was wait and hope that she would call me when I didn't show up.

I was already tired and emotionally stressed over what I now refer to as "my spiritual crisis," so this dilemma pushed me over the edge. I sat in my car with the windows rolled up and in extreme frustration I screamed, "I AM SO _ _ _ _ _ LOST!" Then I started to laugh. I realized that I was not just lost in that city, but in my life as well. My friend did finally contact me and directed me to her home. We had an enjoyable visit, but on the way home, to add to the stress, one of my car windows imploded! Hearing a loud bang, I quickly pulled over and looked around just in time to see my rear passenger window begin to crackle and fall into the back seat of my car. There was no one within distance to have thrown something, so I couldn't imagine what had happened. When I asked the car mechanic about it, he told me it was most likely a "stress fracture."

## Divorced

On June 2, 2004, I got divorced. Although Roger seemed to be moving forward with his life, we both still had strong feelings for one another. If our conversations were ever strained, it seemed to be due to sadness, not anger. Having already lived on my own for two years, I agonized whether it was necessary to divorce him or not. Neither of us was looking to remarry at that point. I wasn't even dating. Part of me intuited that it wasn't necessary to get divorced, but I finally decided that doing so would make a clear statement to the universe that I intended to move forward with my life. We used a mediator to facilitate the legal proceedings. There was no fighting. We had amicably separated our physical belongings long ago.

We had also set up and instituted a financial support agreement that closely resembled what the court ordered. We actually drove into town together for the proceedings and then had breakfast together afterward. I would eventually come to know that, other than making a statement, the divorce was completely unnecessary. It only ended up complicating matters two years later. But, once again, I had made the best decision possible based on what I felt was right at that time.

Although 2004 had been a challenging year, I still felt an ever-deepening sense of wonder and awe that there was much more to life than what I could perceive with my five senses. The synchronicity was becoming even more apparent and I was beginning to pay more attention to what it was trying to tell me. I also realized that questioning my spiritual beliefs was the best thing that could have happened to me. It forced me to swing the pendulum all the way back to my old, more religious way of looking at life. Instead of suppressing or running away from those old fears and beliefs, I faced them head on, examined them, and discovered that they no longer felt true or held any power over me (at least not consciously). I wasn't certain what the future would bring, but I had fully opened the door to my spiritual growth and the seeds for a whole new way of looking at life were about to be planted.

# Planting the Seeds

## 2005—Mystical Moments

### Synchronicity

In Shirley MacLaine's book, *Sage-ing While Age-ing*, she tells us . . . "(Carl) Jung defined synchronicity as 'any apparent coincidence that inspires a sense of wonder and personal meaning or particular significance in the observer.'" Shirley goes on to say, "By recognizing these synchronistic events, we have a new purpose and meaning for our life because we are living and working with Creation. . . Synchronicity is the connecting link that we have to a nonmaterial and nonphysical reality. . .The person who is aware of the occurrence is by far the best qualified to define and understand and comprehend it, because it is personal, reassuring that person that there is a great and caring intelligence helping his or her destiny . . . When you begin to become aware of the synchronicity of the events in your life, your life takes on a truly magical quality that has nothing to do with logic."

**Paying Attention**

I could have called 2005 the year of synchronicity. I still had no understanding of how these coincidences were happening and I sometimes misinterpreted their messages as a result, but it would be another eight years before I fully understood their source and how to view them. At this point in my life, I was simply fascinated by them.

Because of the increasing regularity of these seeming coincidences, my new mantra had become *pay attention*. One of my paintings led me to a message that further reinforced that idea. The predominantly abstract piece I painted included a rendering of an Oriental decoration that hung in my home. It was a three-inch diameter circle wrapped in Chinese red embroidery floss with a five-inch red tassel and a bronze Chinese character in the middle of the circle. After painting it, I became curious to know the English translation for the Chinese character. I returned to the kiosk at the mall where my mother had bought it to see if I could find out. The kiosk had closed, so I decided to walk around the mall for a while. The very next kiosk was selling Asian ware. I stopped and struck up a conversation with the owner. Since he was Asian, I decided to ask for his help. Taking the decoration from my pocket, I explained that I was hoping to learn the meaning of the Chinese character. I didn't really expect the first person I asked to have the answer. Even if he did, I figured he would say it meant something common such as Happiness, Joy, or Good Luck. To my amazement, the man nodded and, with knowing eyes, he smiled at me and said . . .

"It means *pay attention.*"

## I'm Okay

I couldn't help but pay attention a few days later on the ride home from the veterinarian's office. We had just put our beloved family dog to sleep. Our big black lab, Cobalt, was twelve years old. He belonged to our oldest son, Michael, who was in the Air Force and hadn't been home for two and a half years. It didn't surprise me that Cobalt had waited until halfway through our son's month long visit to show symptoms of a terminal illness. I believe he waited to say goodbye to his very best friend. Cobalt was only given two weeks to live. A few days after Michael left, Roger, Greg, and I took him for his final ride to the vet. It was time to let him go.

As we left the office with heavy hearts, the thought suddenly popped into my mind that I would be given a sign that Cobalt's spirit was at peace. I didn't have to wait long. As Greg drove toward home on a quiet country road, a big, beautiful, vibrantly healthy dog came running out into the street, seemingly from nowhere. He sat down right in the middle of the road. Greg had to bring the car to a complete halt while the dog sat there staring at us. He stayed long enough to look each of us directly in the eye before he bounded away. Even my husband who was a skeptic about such things had to comment, because this wasn't just *any* dog. My husband turned toward the back seat where I was sitting and rolled his eyes as he exclaimed . . .

"And it was a black lab!"

## Health Crisis

Shortly after Cobalt passed, I experienced a health crisis of my own. It had been three years since I moved out on my own and life was good. I felt settled in my apartment and had turned it into a lovely home. I maintained a strong connection with Roger and both of my sons. I had wonderfully supportive friends, both old and new, and I was getting by financially. I think my mom could finally see that I was happier than I had been in a long time. I believe that made it a little easier for her to accept my divorce. She and Roger remained close and I wouldn't have wanted it any other way. She could see that I was going out more and having great fun dancing. In fact, I was starting to have more fun than I had had in years!

That is when my health problems began. I was experiencing heart palpitations and a debilitating lack of energy. I could barely put one foot in front of the other. I felt as if there was a cavernous hole in my stomach and a feeling of enormous pressure in my abdomen. I didn't know what was wrong and I was scared to death. I sat in the doctor's office and choked back sobs as I told her, "I haven't been to the doctor in years, I'm *never* sick. I don't know what's wrong, but I feel like, at any minute, I'm going to die!" Hearing my desperation, she scheduled a series of tests but nothing definitive showed up.

Frustrated, I called a dear lifelong friend and told her what was happening. She is an exceptional nurse and I wanted her insight, which I got, but not in the medical context I expected. "How can this be happening to me now?" I asked. "My life was going so well. I was having a blast!" Her answer shocked me. "Paula," she said gently, "Are you having *too* much fun?"

"What do you mean?" I replied.

"You've always felt guilty about leaving Roger," she said. "You not only left him, but now you're having fun too?! Do you think that you don't deserve to enjoy yourself? That you have to suffer for what you did?" She went on, "And sometimes I wonder who you are trying to convince when you say how wonderful your life is. Yes, we can all see that you are happier on your own, but you can't tell me that you don't occasionally have days where you just want to scream and cry and tell the world how sad and angry you are and to just say this day sucks!"

I couldn't respond. I was too busy crying. She was absolutely right. Yes! I felt guilty. Yes! I felt I should be punished. Yes! I was sad, but most of all, I was angry. In fact, I was filled with rage. Why did being true to myself have to be so HARD? Why did it have to hurt other people? I felt the anger surge up from my toes. My friend's words had given me permission to feel and admit all the fear, pain, sadness and anger I had tried to suppress for so many years. They came flooding to the surface in a torrent of tears. It took me by complete surprise.

My friend also helped me see that I had been punishing myself financially; that I felt I had to show the world I was *paying the price* for moving out on my own. If guilt seeks punishment, I was doomed to suffer. I believe I unconsciously manifested my poor health so that I was far too fatigued to do my favorite thing . . . dance. It was the perfect punishment. But the gift of that insight was this: If I had created that situation with my own misguided thoughts, then I also had the power to reclaim my health by thinking differently.

It was a slow, gradual process, but over the next few months, I began to do just that. It was a major step in recognizing the power of the conscious (and unconscious) mind. By excavating crippling old beliefs, I could see how they affected me negatively and then choose healthier new thoughts to replace them. I began reciting affirmations to myself such as, *I am healthy and strong*, *I deserve to be happy*, and, *It is safe to be me*. But it would still be a long while before I came to a different view about how I thought I had "hurt" people by following my heart.

Another unexpected gift arose from my health crisis. After spending an afternoon in the emergency room hooked up to heart monitors, I was sent home, in spite of my protests. The doctors couldn't find anything substantial enough to warrant admitting me. While trying to fall asleep that night, my heart began beating wildly again and I was extremely short of breath. I kept telling myself that the doctors said I was okay, but I was so scared that I had the phone in my hand ready to call 911. I even called out loud for Jesus to help me. I had never done anything like that before. When I called out to Him, I was surprised that the next thought that entered my mind was of the Beatles' song "Let it Be." The lyrics brought the Blessed Mother to my mind. I suddenly felt her calm, loving presence enfold me. Instantly, my heart rate slowed to normal, my breathing became regular and I fell into a deep, peaceful sleep. The next morning, I recalled the medal that had been given to me over two years earlier. Had the Blessed Mother been watching over me all this time?

That afternoon I felt much better so I went to visit my youngest son so he could show me his new electronic keyboard. As he turned it on, he reminded me that he was really a guitarist and that he only knew how to play one song on the piano. I nearly fell over when he sat down and played "Let It Be."

**A New Name**

A few months later, my health was much improved. I was eager to get back to my routine of working, dancing and painting. I was happy when an opportunity arose to do a solo art show at the local library. It was a large show. I displayed over forty paintings. It was the first time that I advertised a show under my new business name, Spirit Rising. The opening reception was very well attended. I was especially pleased when three friends traveled a long distance to surprise me. They knew I had called my art exhibit "Spirit Rising," but none of them knew of my secret desire to someday take a Native American name for myself. When we got together a few months later, the poet of the group presented me with a beautifully framed poem she had written. She said the words just "came" to her after seeing my show.

> A dedicated blessing within this name
> Chosen just for Paula Richards
> The universe shining through
> As she discovers her life's mission
> Now another step she shall take
> Upon the white light path
> Always being known as
> "Spirit Rising."
>                         Daneen Noyes

I could not stop staring at the poem. There it was in writing. I felt I had been given my Native American name!

## Soaring In Sedona

The importance of having a Native American name stems back to many years earlier when a friend invited me to go to a powwow. I went out of mere curiosity, but when we arrived I was shocked. The beads and feathers, the smell of leather and feel of the animal pelts, and the beautiful native jewelry all felt so familiar to me that I didn't quite know what to make of it. The tinkling sound of a necklace I tried on instantly transported me back to an unknown time and place when I was an infant safely cradled in someone's arms inside a teepee. I could hear the rhythmic pounding of drums in the distance, just as I was hearing them at the powwow that day. It felt like they were calling me home. I went from booth to booth that day, buying artifacts, buying distant memories, and feeling like I was buying back pieces of my soul. Each time I go to a powwow, I feel that same familiar wave of inner peace and comfort, a distinct feeling of coming home.

I suspected that I would feel the same way about Sedona, Arizona. With its red rock formations, Native American culture and its reputation as a spiritual center, Sedona had been calling my name for years. Little did I know that a return trip to the library to pick up something I had left there *by mistake* would lead me there. While at the library, I decided to search for a travel book about the southwest. The very first one I picked up just *happened* to be about sacred sites in Sedona.

All morning, I pored over the travel book, noting places I wanted to visit someday. That afternoon, when my friend Mary came to visit, she suggested that I pull an angel oracle card for advice about my health. The card I pulled said, "This situation is perfect. Dive right in. No further research is necessary. DO NOT PROCRASTINATE AT ANY COST!" I immediately and intuitively knew that this was in reference to my going to Sedona. I had just finished telling Mary about the travel book. She picked it up, let it fall open randomly and began reading. "The desert will lead you to your heart where I will speak." I was stunned. Then she told me that just the day before, our friend, Joanne, said to her, "Paula needs to go to Sedona." And a few days before that my friend Dave had told me, "I don't think you'll be truly happy until you go to Arizona."

"Mary," I said. "I can't go to Sedona! How am I going to pay for it?" I could have charged the trip, but that was *not* how I lived my life. I had no means to pay off the card so it was something I was very uncomfortable doing. She suggested that I select another angel card and ask about finances. The first one I pulled out of forty-four cards on various topics said, "I am the Angel of Abundance. You will receive the money that you need, and God is in charge of how that will happen. Have faith."

Okay, I was being shown that I would be alright financially, but I was still concerned about having enough physical energy to make the trip. I was also afraid of traveling alone. I wasn't afraid of flying, but I was not a well-traveled person and I was terrified of getting lost in an airport or any place else for that matter. At the same time, I knew with certainty that I had to go to Sedona alone because it would be a spiritual journey for me. I needed to be able to follow my inner guidance and change my plans at a moment's notice without concern for anyone else's agenda.

Two days later, I decided to stop at Triple AAA Travel Agency just to ask a few questions and get a price estimate. *Who am I kidding?* I thought again. *I can't afford to do this.*

*The desert will lead you to your heart, where I will speak.*

Those words kept burning in my brain. Suddenly I thought *I can't afford NOT to do this!* So I did something that I normally never would have done. I pulled out my credit card, handed it to the agent and said, "Book it!" Even though my health was poor and I was afraid of traveling alone, whether the extra money showed up or not....

I was going to Sedona.

Once I found the courage to set the wheels in motion, the universe supported my plan in the most surprising ways. At the art gallery where I worked, a beautiful sculpture of a Native American woman was delivered to us *by mistake*. The title of the sculpture was "Sacred Calling." And just a few days before my trip, I met a friend at a local bookstore. When I asked how she was doing, her face lit up. "Great!" she said. "I just got back from Sedona!" In her hands was a bag with all the travel literature that someone had lent to her. She lent it to me.

On September 30, 2005, I left for Sedona. The couple I sat next to on the plane had been married there two years earlier. They recommended shops, art galleries, restaurants and other tourist attractions. As we were talking, I noticed that the lady sitting across the aisle from me was reading a book entitled *Daddy's Little Girl* by Mary Higgins Clark. I had to work hard to keep the grin off my face. I knew my dad was with me and would be every step of the way.

The young woman that I sat next to for the second part of the flight turned out to be an artist from Carmel, California, which is well known for its art. We didn't stop talking during the entire trip. When we landed, I was able to locate my suitcase at the baggage claim in less than a minute and a porter was standing right there to help me lift it off the conveyor belt and escort me to the shuttle area which was very close by. It was all so effortless that I had the distinct feeling that my dad was orchestrating everything from above. I could almost see him smiling.

There were ten of us on the shuttle bus. I was the last to get dropped off, so I got to see each hotel and they seemed to be getting nicer with each stop. As we finally approached my hotel, the driver said, "This is a very nice hotel. Wait 'til you see. You're going to love it." He was right. Truly, he had saved the best for last. When I saw my room I was giddy with delight. Not being a seasoned traveler, perhaps I was easily impressed. A spacious room with ultra-plush carpets and linens? A king size bed? Corian countertops? I never expected anything so luxurious!

Having arrived in Sedona after dark, it was quite a treat to wake up the following morning and see beautiful gardens bordering a golf course that was surrounded by towering red rock cliffs. I was in heaven. I started my week by visiting a nearby place called Talaquepaque (Ta-la-ka-pa-kee) that the couple on the plane told me about. It is a group of shops, galleries and restaurants with Spanish colonial architecture, bubbling fountains and lush greenery everywhere. Wandering through the maze of walkways, curved stairwells and flower-filled courtyards was delightful. It was a crisp autumn day with a cool breeze and warm sunshine. I was torn between exploring the shops or staying outside on the balconies to soak in the sun and listen to wonderful music wafting up from the street. One of the songs I heard was, "I Knew I Loved You" by Savage Garden. I was sure they must have been singing about my initial reaction to Sedona.

There was a greeter's booth at the entrance to Talaquepaque. That's where I met Martha. Right away I had a good feeling about her, so I told her a bit about myself and why I came to Sedona. I asked if she had any advice for me. Besides directing me to points of interest within the shops, she pulled out a brochure and said, "This is the man you want to see!" The man was a masseur and spiritual counselor. It turned out that Martha's advice, on the very first morning of my stay, led me to an encounter that was to be the highlight of my trip. She was also emphatic that I did not need to go to the Grand Canyon on this trip. She said, "Stay here in Sedona. This is where the energy is." This confirmed that my thoughts were on the right track. Even though going to the Grand Canyon seemed liked an obvious choice because it was so close by, each time I thought about going, I felt as though I was being pulled away from where I needed to be.

Later, when I called the counselor Martha had recommended, he graciously offered me his services at a discounted rate which exactly matched what I would have spent on the canyon tour. Also, the only appointment time he had open was on the same afternoon the tour had been scheduled. Great confirmation. I would see him in three days.

The next day I was scheduled to take a "Mystical Tour" of Sedona. Each place we visited was said to contain a powerful vortex of energy that could have a very uplifting, long-lasting effect. I certainly found this to be true for myself. My meditations became much deeper while there and, in spite of jet lag, higher elevations and my lingering health problems, I had no trouble climbing to a very high plateau in order to take in the view. This increased energy remained with me throughout the trip.

At the end of my tour I had a Tarot card reading by one of the tour guides. He began by emphasizing that I needed to release my artwork; that my emotional ties to my paintings were keeping them from selling. He reminded me that they were not really mine; that they come through me and need to be released into the world to help heal others. He said new employment was coming and that it would be selling my own artwork. He also explained that I was having hearing difficulties because this was a time for me to learn how to listen to my "inner voice." I was told that romance was coming. "You will meet someone who is a gentleman and a gentle man," he said. To my delight, he was absolutely right. The reader said there was no further need for doctors at that time, which also turned out to be correct. I was especially interested when he told me that I had made all the right choices and "leaps of faith" necessary for spiritual success. He said that, if I hadn't, I probably would have had to deal with some serious health problems, perhaps even mental illness.

The following day I ventured out to promote my own artwork. At the first gallery I visited, the owner immediately approached me, asked if I was an artist and whether I had any work to show him. I thought to myself, *It can't be that easy!* And of course, it wasn't. I had no success there or at any other gallery. I spent the second half of the day shopping and wondering if I had wasted my time that morning. That night, as I was reading *Lucky Man*, by Michael J. Fox, I came across this passage. "It wasn't for me to fret about time or loss but to appreciate each day, move forward, and have faith that something larger was at work, something with its own sense of time and balance." I was very grateful for that reminder.

The following morning, my watch stopped working. I couldn't help thinking it was connected to my meeting with the spiritual counselor that afternoon. I had a feeling that he was going to time warp me right out of this world. In a sense, he did. My session with him left me feeling like I had walked through a gateway into a whole new life. Through his healing work, which included, but was not limited to, age regression and massage with hot rock therapy, I felt like I had communed with the pure essence of love, joy, and laughter. When he asked me to look into his eyes, I literally thought I could see eternity. Simultaneously, I was able to experience all my loved ones who had passed on lovingly looking back at me! And the massage was like nothing I had ever experienced. I could easily have been convinced that I left his office in a different body than the one I had arrived in. It took a long time after that for me to find any words at all to describe what transpired without feeling like I had diluted the experience. It was truly beyond words.

My last full day in Sedona found me taking my first hot air balloon ride. We were up and out at 5:30am for a gorgeous sunrise flight. The weather was perfect and the scenery was spectacular. The wind was calm enough that we were able to fly within twenty feet of huge, sun-drenched rock formations. The quiet was palpable. I felt like I was One with God. When we landed, we had a continental breakfast which included fresh fruit, an assortment of deliciously moist muffins, and a champagne toast. Following my transformational meeting with the healer, and now my balloon flight, I was pleasantly surprised to read the *Balloonist's Prayer*.

The wind has welcomed you with softness.
The sun has blessed you with warm hands
You've flown so high and so well that
God has joined you in laughter,
and set you gently back again
into the loving arms of Mother Earth.

*Author unknown, believed to have been adapted*
*from an old Irish sailor's prayer*

Back at the hotel, I spent the afternoon strolling the grounds of the resort. If I had never ventured off that property, the week still would have been well spent. All my anguish over whether I should have taken the trip was put to rest as I took in the splendor that enveloped me. Everywhere I looked I was dazzled by an array of intense colors and a sculpted landscape like none I had ever seen before. The play of sunlight and shadow on the red rock cliffs gave them an endlessly changing appearance that held me entranced for hours.

Evening found me in the hotel dining room for one last meal. I laughed when the hostess offered to seat me directly across from a single man and asked if I wanted to sit facing him or not. This led us into a deeper conversation about my week's adventures. In exchange for information about some of the places I had explored, she did a palm reading for me in between showing other guests to their seats. She told me that I would be famous. I chuckled when she said, "Your left hand already knows this, but your right hand hasn't figured it out yet." She suggested avenues I should explore with my art and advised that, when I write my signature, I should underline it for success. I didn't have any success catching the eye of the single man, but that wasn't why I was there. All in all, it was a delightful way to spend my last evening.

The morning of my departure, I woke up laughing. There was no particular reason, I was just laughing and feeling like I was floating in the air, like on the balloon ride. I was euphoric. My mind was full of ideas for my artwork. I could see myself releasing it out into the world, letting the joy I put into it help other people touch joy as well. I felt like there was nothing left for me to do on earth but live in joy. My heart was filled with gratitude and overflowing with unconditional love for this extraordinary life. When I went down to the dining room for breakfast, I guess I shouldn't have been surprised to discover a woman seated right across from me wearing a jersey that had JOY printed in big letters across the back.

The trip to Sedona was a major turning point for me. I gained many insights, conquered many fears, and discovered a deeper level of joy than I had previously been capable of experiencing. It was extremely difficult for me to leave. It wasn't just beautiful scenery I went to see; I went to find a part of me that seemed to be missing. And, it wasn't just beautiful scenery that I left behind. I felt as though I left a piece of my soul. There is no doubt in my mind that I will return. Before my trip, three of my friends gave me journals. The guidance was clear. Write everything down.

I did.

# Growing the Garden

## 2006—A Pivotal Year

### Western Avenue Studios

My trip to Sedona may have been one of the most significant weeks in my life, but 2006 was one of the most significant years. In late 2005, I became aware of a nearby mill building that had been converted into art studios. The fifth floor was fully occupied, but now they were opening up another floor. I was very interested in renting a studio there, but I was worried about the cost. When my friend Mary offered to share the space, I placed a deposit to hold a space and prayed that I would be able to pay for it by the time the construction was finished. A month later, still worried about the money, I left an e-mail and a phone message for the landlord letting him know we were pulling out.

In January, my mom asked me when I was moving into my new studio. I reminded her that I had decided not to take it. It was especially difficult to tell her that, since my finances had unexpectedly improved and I could now afford it. I was surprised and delighted to get an e-mail the following morning from the landlord, asking me when I was going to pick up my key and move in. He never received my cancellation messages! I was even more delighted when I discovered that the space we had selected was number five. Because I was born on 5-5-51, and the number five had begun showing up a lot in my life, I had begun using it as a sign of guidance. I saw it as confirmation that I was meant to be there.

## Making My Heart Sing

A while ago, another friend had suggested that I needed to find a church that "makes your heart sing." I hadn't belonged to or even been inside a church for years. I definitely was *not* looking for a religious affiliation or identity, or even a sense of community, but something about that guidance resonated with me so I occasionally found myself stopping to visit churches at random to see if I felt moved by anything. Although I enjoyed the quiet and loved the architecture, no particular church stood out for me.

Around that same time, I found myself accompanying Mary on some errands. I was surprised when she stopped at a local church to purchase something at their gift shop. She told me how beautiful the church was and invited me to go inside with her. The enormous building was exquisitely detailed. The rich colors of the stained glass windows, backlit with sunshine, mesmerized me. A deep sense of sacredness and peace engulfed me as I walked toward the front of the church. As I got closer to the altar, I set eyes on a statue of the Blessed Mother Mary. I found that I couldn't bring myself to turn away. Her serene face and the graceful folds of her pale blue robe were elegantly carved. Her halo was lit with very tiny, sparkling white lights. I know that makes it sound commercial, but it wasn't. It was the most beautiful statue I had ever seen. I knelt in front of her and was suddenly overwhelmed with a sense of peace, safety and love like I had never experienced. It washed over me so quickly and enveloped me so completely that I burst into tears. I didn't care who heard me. I simply wept with joy.

## Johnny O

More joy was on the way. One night at the dance, after once again declining a date by saying that I would only see men at the dances, the man replied, "Well, I guess that's okay if it's enough for you, but you might want to consider that you are missing out on a lot. Sooner or later, you are going to want more." It had been four years since I moved out on my own and when I left the dance alone that night, for the first time, I felt really lonely. I knew it was time to open up to the possibility of a new romantic relationship.

Actually, for quite some time, I had been sensing that I was going to meet someone. I thought I was going to reconnect with a boy I dated in high school. I first got that notion after my psychic neighbor told me that I was going to meet someone whose name began with "J" that I had dated long ago. For two years I had been on the lookout for him. I didn't really have any romantic feelings for him. I just wondered what he would be like after all those years. My neighbor kept talking about someone with the letter "J." "He's going to dance with you," she said. Then she fluttered her eyes and waved her hand in a manner that suggested that it was going to be very romantic. Who wouldn't be curious?

In late April, I did meet someone at the dance whose name began with "J." The very first time Johnny and I danced, it was magical. I had never danced with anyone who moved with such grace. Together, we glided across the floor. We were so perfectly matched that someone actually asked us that first night how long we had been dancing together! I used to watch Johnny dance from a distance. The way he swayed, I could see that he really felt the music, and I often thought how lovely it would be to dance with him. I assumed that he and the woman he was always with were a couple. I was thrilled to discover that they were just good friends.

Over the next few months, I saw Johnny more and more often, both at the dances and at my home. He was easy to talk to and had a wonderful outlook on life. I was enjoying his company, but I had a big concern. I still had it in my mind that I was supposed to reconnect with my old boyfriend. My friend kept saying that maybe Johnny was the letter "J" who the psychic had referred to, but I wouldn't hear of it.

Johnny was very different from the person I imagined having for a romantic partner. We danced amazingly well together, but I still thought that he was *not my type*. I thought for sure that I would be with someone who talked and read about spirituality all the time like I did; someone who was soft spoken, quiet and calm. Instead, although he was a gentle man, Johnny was extremely talkative and had very high energy. About the same time we met, a catchy new song came out by KT Tunstall called "You're Not the One for Me." I had to laugh because my own thoughts were being mirrored back to me in such an amusing way. But another part of me was singing a different tune. One night, as Johnny was twirling me across the dance floor, I found myself staring at him and thinking, *My old boyfriend better show up soon because I think I'm falling in love with this man.*

In spite of my initial resistance, Johnny and I continued dating. We had met in May. That July we attended the Lowell Folk Festival together. Having spent the last few years going places alone most of the time, I was thrilled to have such a delightful companion. We discovered that we were perfect partners off the dance floor as well. We spent all three days together, strolling around, enjoying the food, the crowds, music and, of course, the dancing. At one point, we stopped right in the middle of the cobblestone street to dance to the song, "New York, New York." We soon collected a crowd of onlookers. Being the showman that he is, Johnny ended the dance by dipping me very low. Then we walked away as the crowd cheered. I couldn't remember the last time I had so much fun. It was one of the sweetest weekends of my life.

There was that word again. Was I having too much *fun*? I guess so, because shortly after that, I made a decision to stop seeing Johnny. I decided that I couldn't trust that the *other woman* he still occasionally danced with was only a friend.

## Self-employed

In the midst of this confusion about romantic relationships, I dealt with an unexpected change in my working status. The gallery where I worked for five years closed in August. I was out of work. I had sensed big changes coming within the company, but the closing took me by surprise. For the first time in my life, I began collecting unemployment insurance benefits. I began a job search, but my heart wasn't in it. I was thoroughly enjoying having more time in my art studio and didn't really want a new job.

The unemployment center offered classes on small business development. I woke up one morning with the realization that I needed to stop seeing myself as unemployed and consider myself *self*-employed instead. I was so excited that I jumped out of bed. I dressed in a business casual outfit, dusted off a briefcase I had bought long ago and headed to the career center to start pursuing my dream. I signed up for classes and registered my business name at City Hall. After opening business accounts, I ordered new business cards printed with the name Spirit Rising.

Originally, Spirit Rising was the name of one of my paintings. I eventually chose it as a business name because I thought it sounded uplifting. Also, it was general enough to represent a number of different directions that my business might expand into. Although I was primarily marketing my art at that time, I had a strong sense that I would eventually offer other services. The name also had a strong Native American feel that suited me well.

My layoff became a blessing in another way as well. Little did I know how important it would be for me to have that free time. For months I had told my co-workers and friends that I felt September would be a pivotal month for me and that I needed to "just sit tight and see what happens."

Soon, through a tip from a fellow Toastmaster, an unexpected opportunity came my way to interview a very influential, spiritual leader in my community for a highly regarded magazine. I was excited about the idea, but also scared. I thought, *Who am I to be writing for a big magazine like this?* I discussed it with my friend, Kathy, over a cup of coffee. She said that I needed to use my voice; that people needed to hear what I had to say. I kept saying, "Yeah, but . . . " After about my fifth, "Yeah, but," Kathy launched into a more intense version of, "People need to hear what you have to say." No matter how many excuses I came up with, over and over, she said, "It doesn't matter." Her body language and the look in her eyes had changed in a way I had never seen before. She was, at once, both calm and very insistent. At one point when I tried to interrupt, she blurted out, "This isn't ME talking. You need to listen!" I'm not sure which one of us was more surprised.

Kathy had never channeled information from the spirit world before, but clearly something new and unusual was happening to her. Or should I say *through* her? She seemed to be receiving information from a source outside herself, hearing thoughts that weren't her own. She had a few more messages to deliver to me before she finished. At first she seemed a bit shaken by the experience, but when it happened again later in our conversation, she seemed more at ease with the process. At one point she even giggled, looked up toward the ceiling, and asked, "Is there anything else or are we done?" I felt honored to have been there for my friend's first encounter with channeling information from spirit. I was also grateful for the encouraging messages I had received about my ability to write the article. I went home and placed a call to accept the job but I never got to do the interview. The universe had something else in mind

**September 19, 2006.**

Ring . . . . . . . I stopped writing in my journal.

Ring . . . . . . . *Who'd be calling at 7 a.m.?*

Ring . . . . . . . The caller ID says Lowell General Hospital . . . *Not good.*

I knew in my mind that it was about my ex-husband.

"Is this Paula?"

"Yes," I said, the words, *OH GOD* already screaming in my brain.

"Your husband has been in a very serious motorcycle accident. You need to come right away."

Somehow, I already knew that it was fatal.

"Is there anyone you can bring with you?" . . . . . . . . *Confirmation.*

My friend Mary and I were planning to go to our art studio early that morning, so I knew she was ready and available to come with me. She lived right across the street from my apartment. I chose to drive my own car and have her follow. As I drove I felt all the expected emotions, the shock, fear, panic, grief and disbelief, but somewhere deep below the surface of that emotional storm, I could hear a small inner voice saying, *You're okay. Everything is as it is supposed to be.* I didn't understand it, but the thought persisted.

When we arrived at the Emergency Room, they were still trying to resuscitate Roger. I sensed that this was merely for my benefit and they called off the code soon after we arrived. Before they did, I cried out to him . . . how I loved him . . . what a good father and husband he had been. *How do you sum up thirty-five years of love in a few unprepared sentences?* I pleaded, "Wherever you are, please don't be frightened." I was shocked when, from either side of me, Mary and a nurse both said, "He isn't!"

"He isn't?" I asked.

"NO!" they both responded. I turned to see Mary's serene face and smiling eyes looking back at me. Her words felt beyond questioning and a deep sense of comfort descended on me. When I turned back to Roger, I saw what I had missed before. He looked peaceful.

As Mary and I walked out of the hospital that morning, she said something that totally changed my view of the accident. The information seemed to come to her unexpectedly. I believe that it came from spirit. With sudden insight, she blurted out, "Paula! Roger didn't die because you left him. He let you leave him because he was going to die!" That insight probably saved me years of guilt and psychotherapy.

As I drove away from the hospital, oddly enough, I had a sudden urge to turn on the car radio. The first words I heard were the lyrics from the Sophie B. Hawkins song, "As I Lay Me Down."

> "As I lay me down to sleep,
> this I pray

that you will hold me dear.
Though I'm far away,
I whisper your name into the sky
 and I will wake up happy."

   I don't know how I drove home. Heart wrenching
sobs exploded from me when I heard those words.
There was no doubt in my mind that Roger was
reaching out to me, comforting me, reassuring me that
he was at peace. I didn't feel peaceful in that moment. I
just felt intensely and emotionally connected to the
man I had loved so deeply for all those years; the man I
never stopped loving, even when I knew I had to move
on; the man I still referred to (out loud and in my
heart) as husband, even though we were divorced; the
man who had loved me so beautifully that his death
broke my heart into a gazillion pieces; the man who
gave me the wings to fly. Those timely lyrics became
my lifeline. They let me know what I most needed to
know – that Roger was at peace. I read them, spoke
them, or sang them everywhere I went, to whomever
would listen. I prayed that the song would give others a
sense of peace about his death too.
   I returned to the emergency room with our
youngest son, Greg. Shortly after that my mother met
us there. That was when it occurred to me that, being
the careful driver Roger was, someone else
probably involved in the accident. I learned that the
accident was the result of a collision with a seventeen-

year-old boy driving an SUV. Ironically, it was the same make of car that I was driving. I couldn't help wondering if that was symbolic of my own fear. *Had the anguish I believed I caused my husband led him to a state of mind that was distracted and distraught enough to cause an accident?* That's why Mary's words that morning were so important to me. I clung to them like a life raft.

Although it was never proven *without a doubt* in court, the initial report was that the boy, while making a left hand turn at a traffic light, accidentally cut Roger off. I will probably never know for sure, but it doesn't really matter. Instead of being angry, my heart went out to him. I hadn't met him, but I couldn't help thinking what an awful burden that could be for him to live with.

Months later, when my inner guidance told me the time was right, I sent him a letter. I introduced myself, gave him my contact information should he ever want it, and offered my forgiveness. I didn't actually feel that there was anything that needed forgiving. By that time in my life, I understood that there were no *accidents*. I believed that everything was happening according to a plan much larger than I was able to see or understand. I offered forgiveness only because I thought the *boy* might think he needed it.

The last time I saw Roger was the night before his passing. At my request, we met a friend of mine at a local 99 Restaurant for advice about Roger buying out my share of our house. The meeting was tense as we both struggled with our own set of financial fears. Nothing was settled that night. As Roger gathered his paperwork to leave, his demeanor suddenly changed completely. He went from tense and reluctant to appearing calm and relaxed, almost casual. I will never know what he was thinking, but as he turned to say goodbye, his carefree expression seemed to say, *none of this is going to matter anyway.* With a gentle smile and a twinkle in his eyes, he looked straight at me and spoke these final words . . .

"See ya."

Although there had been some tension between us as we went through the difficult process of separating, Roger and I had a beautiful life together for many years. There is no way, in just a few words, that I can sum up all that our thirty-six year relationship meant to me. As a tribute to how wonderful Roger was, I would like to share a letter he wrote one Christmas.

Dear Santa,

My list is very short this year. There are no things that I really need or want.

There is no big ticket item at the department store that will fulfill my every wish, for my wishes don't plug in or run on batteries. What I already have is far better.

My family is safe and healthy. My wife has discovered a fountain (of artistic expression) within herself that keeps her step quick and her eyes smiling, and is sharing what flows from it with everyone she meets. My sons are becoming the people we thought we might only hope for, with their own direction and purpose and kindnesses to others. Everywhere they go, someone feels a little better for having met one of these people.

So my wants are simple, Santa. I ask for just one thing. Please let others have what I've had. Let them understand that peace comes from within, and shows up as caring for others. That will make my Christmas even merrier.

Thanks,

Roger

**A New Perspective**

Of course, many, *many* people besides me were profoundly affected by Roger's passing, most notably our two sons and daughter-in-law. Informing them of his death was the hardest thing I've ever done. It was early morning and they were all still asleep, one only two miles away, and two out in New Mexico. I cannot speak for them, but I imagine it was the worst wake-up call they ever got.

For me, Roger's death provided the backdrop to help me see more clearly who I was and just how far I had come on my spiritual journey. Although I was deeply saddened in the ensuing days and months, there was a prevailing sense of order, of things falling into place. In the days that followed his accident, I found myself assuming the role of comforter more often than not. And in spite of all the commotion and upheaval, I continued to experience an underlying sense of calmness and a feeling that everything was happening according to some master plan.

That didn't mean that I was in any way okay with him dying. I just had an inner knowing that life and death were following their natural course and that I would be alright. I prayed that the rest of my family, and his, would be as well.

Over time, I was able to look back and see some unexpected blessings in my having left Roger and, perhaps, why so many things had to happen the way they did. Through my leaving, Roger and I experienced the unconditional love that we still had for each other more deeply than ever before—him by graciously letting me go, even though he didn't want to, and me by consoling him when a new relationship of his didn't work out. Roger had taken care of me in many ways over the years. If I hadn't left him when I did, I would not have been as strong and secure as I needed to be for our children when he died. I would not have rented the art studio and established my own business. I wouldn't have gone to the singles dances and met Johnny. Also, if I had stayed with Roger, he probably would not have met the woman with whom he shared the last year and a half of his life. She loved motorcycles as much as he did and they often went on weekend riding trips together. It appeared to me that Roger did more living during that short period of time than he and I had done together over the last fifteen years.

And Mary's words kept coming back to me. *Roger didn't die because you left him. He let you leave him because he was going to die!* Although he could not consciously have known of his impending death, did Roger unconsciously act in ways that prompted me to leave him? Did he push me out of the nest and help me to fly on my own? Because the accident occurred shortly after I began feeling safe, happy and settled, and because of his most unusual behavior at the restaurant the night before his death, I couldn't help but entertain those questions.

No matter why, when or how the accident happened, it is never easy to lose a loved one. I fully acknowledge and respect the anguish that people suffered (and suffer still) from Roger dying. We *all* suffered. But I do believe that, in spite of what *we* might see as unfinished business of the deceased, the soul knows when we have accomplished whatever we came to experience, and that no death is considered premature in the realm of spirit.

**The Berkshires**

Another series of events became clear to me after

118

Roger's passing. Almost two years earlier, I had signed up for a two night vacation in the Berkshire Mountains as part of a time-share marketing plan. I had never done that before. I detested the thought of listening to a sales pitch or taking advantage of the opportunity with no intention of buying anything. But when the phone salesman mentioned horseback riding in the fall foliage, it sounded too good to pass up. I love horses and autumn is my favorite season. I had a whole year to book the vacation, but I procrastinated until it was too late and threw the paperwork away.

A few months later, the man called again. He said that for just twenty dollars, I could re-instate the deal. Once again, I said yes, but this time my decision was a more intuitive one. I felt that this opportunity had come up again for a reason, though I didn't know why. I booked a room for two days in early October, just before the plan was about to expire. Then Roger died. Going to the Berkshires was the last thing on my mind.

When Greg and I picked up my older son and his wife at the airport for the funeral, we were happy to learn that they would be home for two full weeks. Suddenly, I remembered the vacation package. The two nights I had scheduled in the Berkshires coincided with the last two nights of their visit and the suite I had booked would sleep four people. The four of us enjoyed a much needed vacation together for free. It was a wonderful way to end an exhausting two weeks and, because of Roger's recent death, I had a legitimate reason to tell the salesperson that I couldn't make a big financial decision at that time.

## Jarod is Here

Another gift came my way in the late fall. For a number of years I had attended a spiritual discussion group at Borders Bookstore. Over a period of many months, I witnessed a significant change in one of the group members named Maria. Each week I saw her, she seemed to be more and more peaceful, composed and self-assured. She also looked younger and healthier. When I commented on it, she said she had been taking some "breath work sessions" with a man named Jarod. I had heard his named mentioned before and always with high praise for his work. He had spoken to the group months earlier, but I was unable to attend. After seeing my friend's transformation, I was interested in experiencing the breath work sessions for myself, but it was a very long drive to Jarod's house and the sessions were more costly than I could justify investing in at that time.

On this particular evening, as soon as I arrived at the bookstore, I had the distinct feeling that Jarod was there. I didn't know what he looked like, but as I browsed the store before the meeting, I kept looking around trying to imagine which person was him. When I went upstairs to join the group, I discovered that there was another speaker scheduled and Jarod wasn't there. I wondered why I had such a strong feeling about meeting him.

After the meeting, my friend Maria approached me to ask a favor. She said she had been taking lessons from Jarod to become a breath work instructor. She wanted to know if she could practice on me! The series of six sessions would be held in her home nearby and they were free. Not knowing about my earlier expectations to meet Jarod that very night, Maria was startled when I jumped out of my chair and yelled, "YES!"

Coming at a time of such change and upheaval in my life, Maria's sessions proved to be extremely helpful to me. Through a series of lengthy, intense breathing exercises and follow-up discussions with her, I always left her home feeling calm, more centered, and with greater insight into what was going on in my life.

**Mary, Did You Know?**

Life in general had settled down in the three months since Roger's passing and I was trying to deal with getting through the first Christmas holiday without him. I made a trip to his gravesite, an hour's drive away. On the way home, I found myself surfing the radio channels to hear the song, "Mary, Did You Know?" written by Mark Lowry and Buddy Greene. The song had been out for a few years, but this was the first year I had heard it. The beautiful lyrics are about the

Blessed Mother and I wanted to hear its comforting words as I drove home. I channel surfed to no avail.

Although drained from my trip to the cemetery, I decided to attend an "Art and Spirit" program that evening at a local church. I thought it would do me good to get out. The woman sitting next to me in the circle turned out to be the presenter for the evening. I closed my eyes to listen as she began to play her guitar and sing. I was amazed when the first song she sang was "Mary, Did You Know?" Here was this lovely woman with an angelic voice, sitting right beside me, singing the very song I longed to hear. I felt Mother Mary's presence so strongly that, by the time the song ended, my hands were clasped over my heart and I was crying. Judging by the silence in the circle, I think everyone there knew that something special had just happened.

There was another special thing that happened during Roger's wake. I reconnected with a good friend that I had lost touch with over the years. As I saw Cindy enter the funeral home, I wondered how she was doing. *Was she still practicing nursing? Was she still with her husband? Was she well?* My recollection of our conversation in the receiving line was that she told me her husband was terminally ill and I said how sorry I was to hear that.

A few weeks later, she called and thanked me profusely for what I said to her that evening. She said that, instead of her comforting me, she was surprised to find me comforting her. When I hesitated she said, "You probably don't even remember what you said, do you?"

"No, not really," I admitted.

"How did you know that my husband was ill?" she asked. "Had you spoken to one of our nursing friends before I saw you?"

"No," I said. "Why?"

"Because," she said, "when I told you he was sick, you said, 'I know. I will help you.'"

She went on to say that she would never forget the look in my eyes and the warmth in my hug as I said those words. She said it was like nothing she had ever experienced before and she would be forever grateful. I don't remember saying those words. Did she hear what she wanted to hear? Did those words get spoken through me from the spirit world? I don't know. A few months later her husband did pass on. I was right there by her side.


# 2007—Moving Forward

**Two for the Money, Three for the Show**

The synchronicity I had been experiencing since Roger died continued into the following year.

One day when I was feeling particularly sad over losing him, I decided to go sit down by the river. I found it comforting there. As I sat on a bench looking out over the water, I noticed that someone's helmet had washed up near the shore and was lying right in front of me. Roger's helmet had come off during the accident. Across the river I could see the top of the hospital building where he had been taken and the sound of sirens in the distance were an added reminder of that fateful day. I sat staring until the helmet dislodged and floated further downstream.

Later that evening, I had plans to go out to dinner and a Japanese Taiko Drumming performance with my son, Greg. We had found eighty dollars worth of quarters in Roger's piggybank and agreed to set them aside for a special outing together. We were both looking forward to the show, but I was wishing that Roger could be there. During dinner and on the way to the theater, I made a point of reminding Greg that this evening was "on Dad." When we stepped into the auditorium, the first thing I saw brought me to a standstill. On the end seat of the back row there was a yellow and black motorcycle jacket, like Roger's, sitting propped up, looking very much like someone was still in it. There was a helmet resting on the seat beside it. I had no doubt. He was there with us.

Oh, and the cost of dinner and the show? It came to *exactly* eighty dollars.

**Perpetual Motion**

A month later, I visited a local thrift shop to donate some of Roger's belongings. Along with his clothing, I had boxes of house wares, games and other miscellaneous items. I had spent the last few days sorting through his stuff. During this process, I couldn't help but have him on my mind. I missed him and was hoping he was at peace. But, as I packed his belongings, I was also contemplating what new direction my life would take.

I decided to stay and look around the thrift store for a few minutes. Upon leaving, I was surprised to see that one of the items I had just donated had already been put on display. When I thought about what it was, my eyes filled with tears. It was a perpetual motion desktop decoration. As I walked towards the door sniffling, a woman passing by commented that her niece had the sniffles too and she hoped she wouldn't catch them. I replied that she needed to remember to keep picturing herself being healthy because our thoughts create our reality. "You got that right!" she said, and continued, "I have a very intelligent friend and he says that you can do or be anything you want." I walked away smiling; knowing that reminder was sent to me by my own intelligent, *perpetual* friend in the spirit world.

**Off the Wall**

Someone must have been watching over me when I took my newest paintings off the front wall of my studio as well. I had made an appointment to show them to a local restaurant owner the following morning. When I arrived, the restaurant was closed and the owner never showed up. I wasn't able to reach him by phone and he never returned any of my messages. It was as if he didn't exist.

My paintings remained in my car for a few days because I had other commitments that kept me from going back to my studio. At an art event a few evenings later, one of my colleagues asked me how much damage was done to my artwork. When I looked puzzled she said, "Didn't you know? There was a spill in the studio above you and brown liquid leaked down your whole front wall. I thought you had removed your paintings because they were damaged." After I got over my initial shock, I smiled. I realized why the appointment with the restaurant owner never materialized. Meeting with him wasn't important. It was all about saving my artwork. I took it as encouragement to keep pursuing my art career.

**The Big Corner Office**

I received greater confirmation in July of 2007 when I moved into a larger art studio. My friend Mary had long since stopped sharing my space with me. I loved having the whole place to myself, but I was considering getting two smaller studios so I could use one as a messy work space and the other as a gallery to show my work.

Around the same time, I received a tip that a larger corner studio would soon become available. It had a huge storage closet that the others didn't have. The closet not only afforded me more space, it jutted out into the room, dividing the studio into two distinct sections; a smaller section up front that was perfect for a gallery and a larger space down back that I could screen off for my work space. And there was still a large center area that was big enough for two long work tables that could seat eight people. It was perfect. The studio had five huge windows affording a lovely view of the nearby canal. There was a wonderful cross breeze and lots of sunshine. It didn't take me long to realize that this wasn't just a place for me to create paintings. This was a gathering space to be shared with lots of people.

Although the larger studio was a bit more expensive, I quickly got confirmation that this was a good move for me. During the week I moved in, I received many free items to help me set up my new space. From multiple sources, I received a mini refrigerator, a fan, an upholstered chair, shelving for my storage closet, a desk, a decorative storage cabinet, and a mini microwave for just $10.

Johnny, who I had reconnected with at the dances, ran a handyman business. He helped me scrape and paint the twelve-foot high walls and hang curtains and shades. He built screens for the huge windows and performed many other small jobs. Thanks to Johnny, within a few weeks we had created a warm, welcoming space that I could hardly wait to share with the world. I finally felt like I was in business.

## Birthing Spirit Rising

I chose Spirit Rising for my business name quite a while ago, but I wasn't clear what my business *was* until I moved to the larger studio. I realized that it was a perfect place for me to hold workshops and informal get-togethers that I would eventually call Spirit Gatherings. The inspirational sayings that had so long ago led me to doing calligraphy were now decorating my walls alongside my paintings. I was beginning to see that everything I did, from writing to speaking to creating art, was all focused on lifting people's spirits. And by living *my* dream, I was paving the way for others to live theirs.

## Romance

Another dream coming true for me was Johnny. After I had pulled away from him at the dance, he sent me a card with a beautiful, handwritten note. He ended it with, "Life goes on, being beautiful." His big heart and bright, optimistic spirit shone through in his words. My immediate reaction was, *I think I made a mistake.* Thankfully, a few weeks later, Johnny gave me a second chance. When he asked me to dance, our reconnection was so powerful that I knew instantly that I should never have let him go. Our hearts beating wildly, we spun around and around in joyful celebration.

Because he lived almost an hour away, I mostly saw Johnny on the weekends. Those two days were like a mini vacation which often included fine dining and dancing. I discovered that he was a gentle man of deep wisdom. Although our current life situations only allowed us to be together part-time, our love grew stronger and stronger.

**Oregon**

I also dreamed of doing more traveling. In the previous two years, I had managed to travel to Florida to visit a friend, and Greg and I had visited Michael and Leslie in New Mexico. The four of us had also been to the Berkshires and now I was going with my mom to visit my Godmother and her daughter in Oregon. I was excited to be going someplace new and more distant. When I saw the Pacific Ocean for the first time, I was enthralled with its breathtaking beauty. It was so different from the Atlantic coastline. I marveled at the varied rock formations jutting out of the water. The sun playing off the jagged rocks and the spray from the water crashing around them provided an endless visual display that took my breath away.

I stayed with my Godmother's daughter. We hadn't seen each other for years and I was looking forward to getting reacquainted. It was delightful visiting with her and her husband and touring the area and I thoroughly enjoyed their luxurious home. They lived high on a bank overlooking a lively river. The first morning, I awoke in my private suite to the sound of geese honking as they flew over the water. I poured my coffee and sat on the deck. It was high enough that I was able to look down on the geese flying by. I was surrounded by flowers, sunshine, and chirping birds. There were even hummingbirds at a feeder just a few feet away. As I gazed across the sloping lawn to the willow trees swaying along the river bank and listened to the gentle flow of water in the distance, I felt like I was in paradise. It seemed that, over the last year, life had taken me many special places, each more spectacular than the one before. I believed I was being shown what was available to me in life. I knew I had to dream bigger dreams for myself.

I was beginning to understand how powerful my imagination was. Whatever I put my focus on seemed to expand in my life, especially if I put a lot of emotion behind my thoughts. But I was amazed to see how easily I could slip into a pattern of negative thinking. The secret was to stay positive and imagine whatever I wanted without worrying about how it would come about. I had to get into the mental place of feeling like whatever I wanted already existed. I had to learn how to wish without worrying. When I remembered to do that, the results were amazing.

## Speaking at Borders

One of the things I wanted was to be a motivational speaker. My first big opportunity was a chance to speak at Borders Bookstore. Each month the metaphysical group I attended would have a scheduled speaker on topics ranging from psychic phenomena, to astrology to past lives and more. When I joined the group, I was a bit intimidated by the knowledge and vast experience people seemed to have in "things beyond the physical world." As I grew spiritually, I began to join the discussions more and more and even dared to envision myself as a speaker.

At one meeting, after giving some solicited advice to a friend, she mentioned that the group had a few openings for speakers. "You should sign up!" she said. She went on to say that I had been really helpful to her and that she could see how much the group respected my opinion whenever I spoke. My confidence bolstered, I gave my first presentation to the group two months later. My topic, *Will the Real You Please Stand Up*, was about living an authentic life. The talk was well attended and seemed to be well received. I was hardly nervous at all. In fact, it felt so natural for me to be speaking that I wondered why it had taken me so long to do it.

# 2008—More Growth

### Little Guru

The year 2008 found me happily working in my new art studio. There were now over one hundred and fifty artists in the building. The community was growing very fast and the potential business opportunity proved to be much greater than I had expected. Visitors often commented on how inviting my space was. The brick walls were painted a pale yellow which nicely set off the light brown wicker furniture I had. The huge windows had bamboo shades with gauzy white curtains tied back with rawhide lacing adorned with natural wooden beads. With a cross breeze on a warm day and sunlight streaming in, the room was an inviting oasis. My artwork, combined with motivational sayings on the wall, the lovely décor, and background music, created a space that people found both peaceful and uplifting. It became more and more important to me to cultivate that tranquil feeling for everyone who visited. I knew I was no longer just showing and selling my art. I was creating an experience.

Actually, I was doing a whole lot better at creating an experience than I was at selling my work. People seemed to really like my art, but their interest wasn't translating into many sales. Looking back, I can see that I still had an attachment to my creations. They were like my babies and I wasn't sure I was ready to let them go. I think people subconsciously picked up on that. Also, I had not yet seen the value in my own work and couldn't bring myself to believe I could get paid for doing something I loved to do. It seemed too good to be true and I didn't feel worthy of an easy, abundant life.

I knew this attitude was holding me back and I was getting tremendous guidance from the spirit world that I could be financially successful. One example came from my friend's five-year-old daughter. One day she unknowingly sent me a whole string of messages about abundance. While her mom and I were talking, she was playing "art store." She would not quit until we had purchased every one of her paintings. Then, right when her mom asked me to create a painting of four angels for her, her daughter came over and gave me four pennies. We immediately saw the connection between the four angels and the four pennies. I believed the angels were showing me I could get paid for my artwork. The most notable message occurred when Kathy and I were at her computer sending an email message to my home. Her daughter asked if she could send me a message too. Being only five, she typed gibberish for many lines, except when she stopped and said, "Oh, and this is important!" She then typed $$$$$444444$$$$$$. In the world of numerology, many fours in a row signify that the angels are sending you a message. Here, in the midst of her gibberish, were all these fours surrounded by the symbol for money!

A few days later, my son came over to repay $100 he had borrowed. He pulled a large wad of bills from his pocket and told me he had just cashed three checks at the bank. As he counted the money out into my hands he said, "I don't think I've ever held this many bills before and, interestingly, when I added up the three checks, it came to exactly four hundred and forty-four dollars."

Around the same time, I had developed a series of five motivational seminars. These Spirit Rising Seminars were held at my studio and included topics such as, "Will the Real You Please Stand Up!", "Be Still and Listen", "Dare to Dream", "Pay Attention" and "The World *Wise* Web." These were subjects I had already been talking about with people for a few years. Because I was starting to live my dream, I was becoming a magnet for advice on how to live a more rewarding life. I decided it was finally time to offer some of this information in a more structured format and that my hard-earned wisdom was worth getting paid for. I offered the first seminar in May. Only a few people attended, but it was a beginning. The feedback was very positive and it felt great to get paid for doing something I loved.

## Where is Paul?

After the first workshop in May, I got cold feet. I just could not seem to motivate myself to schedule the next one until I received a call one day from a man named Paul. Since he shared my father's name, I paid extra attention for possible guidance. The man was calling to find out when I was holding the "Dare to Dream" seminar. That was the push I needed. I scheduled it for mid- August on a date that was convenient for the caller. I spoke with him a few more times by phone, but I got the distinct feeling that he wouldn't show up. My instincts were right. He was merely the catalyst to get me moving. What was even more interesting though was what happened when another artist from my building showed up for the seminar. I didn't recognize him immediately so I asked, "Are you Paul?"

"No," he said. "I'm not Paul. But your friend down by the front door and another person in the lobby also asked if I was Paul. No," he explained, "Paul couldn't be here tonight, so I guess I'm standing in for him in spirit." I was grinning from ear to ear. I *knew* that my dad was right there with me, cheering me on.

Another funny thing involving my dad had happened around the same time. After being introduced to the man at the dance who looked like my father, it seemed like I saw him everywhere I went. At first it sort of unnerved me. Was he following me? As I was walking away from an outdoor summer concert that he also attended, I found myself talking out loud to my father's spirit and saying, "I don't get it. It seems like everywhere I go, there he is!" As soon as I said those words out loud, I got it. The man who looked like dad kept showing up to let me know that my father was with me everywhere I went!

**The Trial**

I'm sure he was with me during a particularly difficult time in my life. It had been almost two years since my husband's accident, and the courts were finally conducting the trial for the boy who collided with him. I had been subpoenaed to speak briefly to help the jury relate to Roger in a more personal way, but I would have attended the trial anyways because I wanted to honor him by being there. I also felt it might bring some closure for all of us if I met the boy and his family.

My friend, Kathy, came with me the first morning. Having her there to talk with and keep my mind occupied while we were waiting to begin was an enormous help. The trial lasted two days. The boy and I had no contact until the trial ended, but I did encounter his mother in the ladies' room. With tear-filled eyes, she thanked me for the letter I sent her son. She said it had helped him a lot and that he still had it two years later. I was also happy to hear that he wanted to speak with me after the trial.

The boy was not convicted of a crime. There was too much reasonable doubt. I believed he was probably punishing himself more than any imposed sentence from a judge would have done anyways. When the trial ended, we approached each other with open arms. The fierce, heartfelt hug he gave me told me I was right. We openly wept together . . . for the loss . . . for the pain . . . for Roger. Then, his father embraced me with one of the most comforting hugs I've ever had. Cradling me in his arms, he rocked me back and forth with such love and compassion that I cried harder still.

**Yellow!**

Although I had managed to stay fairly calm and composed through most of the trial, hearing the constant retelling of the accident from many different angles made it seem much more real and like it had just happened yesterday. That and meeting the boy and his family for the first time left me emotionally drained. I knew I needed to nurture myself.

As tired as I was, I kept entertaining the idea of repainting my kitchen. My whole apartment was nicely decorated in neutral tones, but all of a sudden I had an intense need for bright colors. I wanted to paint the kitchen banana yellow, and accent it with white trim and red pottery. My mind kept telling me all the things that I *should* be doing, but my heart was telling me to paint. For three days, I immersed myself in bright yellow as I re-decorated my room. By the time it was done, my mood was elevated and my energy was too. I felt like I had painted a new me.

**Cassie's Reading**

July was full of surprises. A few months earlier, I met a new resident at Western Ave. studios who was not only an artist, but also a published author and writing coach. I had done a bit of writing myself, mostly journaling, but I believed that some of what I had written would someday be part of a book. I felt that I was meant to tell the story of my spiritual journey. I wondered if there was supposed to be a self-help component to it, but I couldn't seem to fit the two together. I sensed that one discussion with Cassie would help me solve this dilemma. She offered to do a Tarot card reading and channel information from my spirit guides.

By this time in my life, I firmly believed that Beings in the spirit world were always with me, guiding me toward my highest good. After quieting my mind, I would ask a question about a certain issue I was dealing with and then wait and watch for answers. Instead of asking specific questions, I might say "The issue is my health (or wealth, or my book, or whatever), what do I need to know right now?" Then, I would pay attention to things I heard and saw and felt. Perhaps I would overhear a meaningful conversation while waiting in the grocery line or someone would give me a book that was helpful or I'd see a billboard sign with a message that resonated with me.

The night before my scheduled reading with Cassie, I sat down and wrote a list of questions I wished to ask my guides about writing my book. When the list was completed, I put it aside and turned on the television. The first thing I saw was an advertisement for a credit card. The sound was muted, but these words were written in bold type across the screen, *What is your story? We'll help you write it.*

**Soul mates**

A big part of my story was my growing relationship with Johnny. It had been two years since we first attended the annual Lowell Folk Festival together. That weekend was sweet because I was just getting to know him and I was exploring the possibility that he was the one for me. This year's festival was even sweeter because I knew that he was the one for me. I remembered the vision I had almost ten years earlier of me walking hand in hand in perfect stride with a man who was exactly my height. It seemed we were linked together, but facing forward, walking through life. There was an unbelievable sense of security, peace and an unquestionable knowing that we were supposed to be together, side by side. In the vision, I could not see the man's face, but now I had no doubt that it was Johnny's.

I used to say that the love we shared was unconditional, but that was redundant. If there are conditions, then what we are experiencing is not love. We may believe that it's love, but it is actually based on what we *need* from the other person. When I decided to leave my husband, I didn't leave him for someone else. I think part of my quest to be alone was an attempt to find the part of me that was already whole and complete. That didn't mean that I would not eventually *desire* to be with someone else. It meant that I didn't *need* someone else in order to be happy. There's a huge difference. Desire is a normal, healthy expectation that we can experience ever-expanding joy in our life. Need, on the other hand, implies that the basis for our happiness resides somewhere outside of ourselves and that we can only be happy if certain *conditions* are met. Unconditional love? What other kind *is* there?

There were certainly times that I was lonely when I began living alone, but there were times that I felt lonely in my marriage as well. I eventually began to understand that the primary relationship I had to have was with myself. If I wasn't happy on the inside, no one and nothing outside of myself could make me happy. At most, they could only give me a temporary, false sense of security. When I *was* happy on the inside, everything in my external world reflected that happiness back to me. And it was when I was able to love myself more *unconditionally* that I attracted a man into my life who could love me that way as well. As with Roger and I, Johnny and I truly wanted each other to be happy, even if it meant having to let the other person go.

**Spirit Gatherings**

The joy that I was experiencing in my relationship with Johnny was spilling over into every aspect of my life. In early August, I scheduled my first Spirit Gathering. These were informal meetings, hosted in my studio, to offer a nurturing space for guests to share uplifting conversation, stories and ideas. The goal was to inspire each of us on what I called our "journey of Spirit Rising." I offered these gatherings for free. It was a way to get people into my studio and introduce them to my work but, more than that, I felt it was a joyful way that I could give back to the surrounding community.

**Letting My Spirit Soar!**

In early September, I was to learn even more about being good to myself. Someone gave me a book by Louise Hay called *You Can Heal Your Life*. I was somewhat familiar with her teachings about how physical ailments can be brought on by our oftentimes faulty thought patterns, but I had never thoroughly read about her philosophy. The main point that I took from her writing was that my level of physical, emotional and spiritual wellbeing correlated to how much I was able to love myself. This wasn't about ego-inflated behavior. It was about a genuine acceptance of myself exactly as I am. And, it wasn't that I couldn't strive to be better, but it began with loving myself now. One of Louise's suggestions was to do what she called "mirror work." It involved looking into my own eyes in the mirror and saying, "Paula, I love you. I love you exactly as you are." The first few times I did this it felt very strange, but it got easier with practice. She also suggested that I tell myself, many times each day, that "I approve of myself." Instead of being hard on myself, she said that I should embrace, love and comfort the small child within me that sometimes felt sad, angry or frightened.

I began doing all those things on a daily basis. I kept a handheld mirror next to my favorite reading chair and used it often. I began practicing saying other things into the mirror as well. I would pretend I was telling my mother how I had just sold a large painting for five thousand dollars or that I went to the doctor for a checkup and all my health problems had disappeared, and so on. I did this consistently for about three weeks. One day, as I gazed into the mirror and began my positive self talk, I noticed a change. There was a light heartedness about myself that I hadn't felt before. In fact, I was almost giddy. I was laughing and smiling and the eyes looking back at me were shining with joy.

This was a major breakthrough for me; a clear demonstration of the power of the mind. It gave me so much hope to think that my life, as I aged chronologically, didn't have to be a downward spiral to illness prior to death. About a year earlier, I had read two books by Marlo Morgan called *Mutant Message Down Under* and *Mutant Message Forever*. In them, she spoke of an Aboriginal tribe that was so spiritually evolved that the members never got ill. They simply chose when they wished to leave the earthly plane. They didn't have to escape into the spirit world during their sleep by dreaming because they were able to slip into a lucid dreaming state during the daytime while they were awake. When they were ready to pass on, they simply chose not to return from their dream. I found this both fascinating and reassuring. It was certainly a state of being worth striving for.

My spiritual growth wasn't a consistent upward swing. I wasn't able to maintain the level of euphoria I felt while looking in the mirror that day. But it showed me a glimpse of what was possible and encouraged me to continue applying Louise Hay's wisdom in my life.

**Healing Touch**

As I continued growing, I learned to ask better questions. Years ago, when I first began to acknowledge that there might be a greater power to tap into, my questions were rather self-centered. They revolved around how I could get what I wanted out of life. Or, I would ask for things for other people that I assumed they needed and wanted. For example, if my friend was sick, I would pray for them to get better. That's what I wanted and what I assumed they needed. I certainly wasn't being selfish in my request. But I believe my prayers were misguided. Then one day, I visited a dear friend in the hospital. She was very, very sick. I thought she might die. We sat and talked briefly, but it quickly tired her out. I told her she didn't have to talk. I would sit there and just hold her hand. As I closed my eyes, I found myself visualizing healing energy flowing from me to her. Then, I sensed Jesus standing over us and realized that the energy wasn't coming *from* me, it was coming *through* me. Suddenly, I knew what to ask. Instead of presuming that my friend needed to get better, I asked that this energy help her to heal *in whatever way was best for her*, even if that meant helping her to die peacefully. Instead of feeling sad, I found myself deeply at peace.

My friend ended up getting well and going home. Months later, when we were discussing my visit with her in the hospital, she told me that she had felt waves of healing energy flowing through her body when I held her hand. She said it was very comforting and peaceful. Although she had enjoyed other forms of healing energy work before, she said she had never felt anything as powerful as what she experienced that day.

That was incredible confirmation for me that there was a greater power than myself at work in the universe. It was not just *outside* myself. It was something I could tap into and allow it to work through me.

## Better Questions

I was finally recognizing that there was a bigger plan evolving than what my mind could imagine. I didn't need to control things and have all the answers. It was more important to have the right questions. Instead of, "How can I get *this* job?" I asked, "What is my divine purpose?" Instead of, "Please take away my pain." I asked, "What do I need to learn so I can let this pain go?" "What can I get?" turned into, "How can I give?" And, "Why did this happen *to* me?" became, "Why did I attract this situation into my life?" or "How can I see this from a higher perspective?" Instead of, "I need things to go *this* way." I asked, "What would be for the greatest good of everyone involved?" "How can I get rich?" switched to, "Help me be open to receiving the perfect amount for me to fulfill my divine purpose."

In Florence Scovel Shinn's book, *The Game of Life And How to Play It*, she says "...man's highest demand is for the *Divine Design of his life . . .* His demand should be: *Infinite Spirit, open the way for the Divine Design of my life to manifest; let the genius within me now be released; let me see clearly the perfect plan . . .*" I came to understand that this perfect plan would always be for the good of all and the harm of none. Whenever I thought of cutting corners or cheating someone else in even the slightest way in order to get ahead, I would remind myself that God is the source of my abundance. No one else had to suffer in order for me to prosper.

I believe that my life was improving so dramatically not only because I was asking better questions, but because I was getting better at paying attention to the guidance coming to me. The more I was open to it, expected it and intentionally asked for it, the more guidance I received. As I mentioned earlier, I believed that one of the ways the angels guide us is by showing us sequences of numbers that correlate with certain messages. There was still a lot I did not understand about the true source of guidance and how to interpret it appropriately, so I allowed it to feature strongly in helping me make an important business decision.

**Spirit Rising, the Shop**

It had been two years since Roger's passing. I had enjoyed the incredible, life-transforming gift of financial security that allowed me to devote myself full-time to my family, my newfound relationship with Johnny, my art and my motivational work. But now I could see my money reserves getting lower and lower and felt that my time of "freedom" was about to end. I reluctantly began thinking that I would have to get a "real job."

My thoughts took a different turn after a conversation I had with a friend about my financial situation. She said that my investments should be making, rather than losing, money. She suggested investing in a less traditional way. "Perhaps in a new business venture," she recommended.

Two days later, while chatting with my friend Mary about investing, she reminded me about a local, spiritually based business that was for sale in the center of a charming, nearby town. At first I was very resistant and said I was looking to invest, not buy a business. Mary countered that I needed to consider investing in myself and this was a great opportunity to further the work I was already doing with Spirit Rising. She suggested that I pull a card from her Angel deck about this situation. Out of forty-four cards, the one I picked talked about a change in direction. I did feel at that time that I had taken my business as far as I could at Western Ave. and that I needed a separate space with more visibility and better accessibility in order to succeed.

The following morning, while running errands, I was quite surprised to find a grasshopper inside my car. It jumped right at me, startling me. When I got home, I checked my *Animal Speak* book by Ted Andrews to see what grasshoppers symbolized. Just as the angels sometimes communicate with us through numbers, I had learned that animals often have messages for us as well. The grasshopper's message was all about taking risks and leaping forward and how I *could* jump into a successful venture. It also encouraged me to listen to my inner voice.

Well, my inner voice was telling me that this opportunity was financially risky, but there seemed to be a lot of synchronicity surrounding the venture as well. Numerical sequences that caught my attention offered messages that spurred me on. For example, one night I noticed that the thermostat in my home was set to 71 degrees, the actual temperature was 71 degrees and the time was 7:11pm. I read that these numbers indicated that I was doing great and on the right path. Later that same night, when I pulled a card from my faerie deck, it said that I couldn't have selected a more auspicious card for starting something new. It also warned not to let my pessimism (or my fear?) cripple me! The oracle cards all seemed to be telling me that something new was being brought into my life and that miracles might happen. They said it was a time for taking action and passing on my blessings and learning through service given from a position of strength.

This was all happening so quickly that I wasn't even really sure what my vision of a business was. But it became clear to me during a week of negotiations that buying out that existing business was *not* the direction I wanted to take. However, if I had not explored the possibility of buying that business, I probably never would have considered looking for a space at all. But now my antennae were up and when a space presented itself a week later, I was ready.

Well, I use the term "ready" rather loosely. Actually, I was scared to death. My biggest fear was that I wouldn't be able to finance and sustain a business on my own. But, once again, I let the synchronicity push me forward. For example, one morning I awoke with the thought that, if I were to open a shop, it would be nice if the phone number ended in 1111 so it would be easy for customers to remember. That afternoon I went to Chelmsford Center to scout around for a location to rent. Someone told me about a space a block away from the business I had originally considered buying out. When I first saw the building, I was undecided about whether to call the realtor. That was until I saw his phone number posted in the window. It was 251-1111.

## Synchronicity Abounds

I signed the lease for the new space in late October. I was delighted to see that the wall color in the new shop complemented most of my artwork extremely well. But what was much more extraordinary was discovering that the inside of the shop looked incredibly similar to a picture postcard I had saved for years. It was an advertisement for a southwestern gallery that I always thought would be the perfect place to show my work. The wall color, the floor color, the wall configuration . . . everything in the shop was almost identical to the picture! More than anything else I had ever experienced, this proved to me the value of creating a vision board and using my imagination to manifest what I wanted. I had stumbled across the postcard a year or two before I ever entertained the idea of opening a shop. I had cut and pasted a few images of my own art- work onto the postcard so it looked like they were part of that gallery. I hung it over my desk where I would see it every day. I never worried about how it would come about. I always felt that it would become a reality in the distant future. I never dreamed that it would materialize so soon and right in a neighboring New England town!

The timing was even more perfect on the morning that I was supposed to get my permit for the outdoor sign. On the way to the town hall, I decided to make a quick stop at my shop. I bumped into another store owner from the same plaza. When I mentioned getting my sign permit, she said, "Oh, so you're going to the meeting tonight?"

I replied, "No, I'm going to the town hall right now."

"Well," she said, "this plaza is in the historical section of town and you have to get permission from the Historical Society for your sign. They only meet once a month and the meeting is tonight!" Since I was trying to open my business in time for the holiday shopping season, this information was crucial for me. The woman phoned her friend at the town hall to make sure he didn't leave the building before I got there because I needed his signature. She then proceeded to tell me how to connect with the Historical Society members to attend the meeting that night.

Everything moved along very quickly after that. My target opening date was just five weeks from the day I had signed the lease; not much time for someone with no business plan or background! But I believed that I was getting tremendous help from spirit because of all the synchronicity that surrounded my efforts. Everything seemed to magically appear at just the right time. I would easily find the items I needed that matched my décor, the product I wanted would be on sale or the right person would show up with the information I needed.

The shop officially opened on December 7, 2008. I was glad I no longer had to run around to different stores, sign shops, insurance agents and the like and could finally have time to just be in the shop and enjoy it. There were still things to be done, but the frenzied pace of the last five weeks was behind me. Now it was time to settle in and see what Spirit Rising was really all about.

# 2009—The Year of the Shop

## Setting Goals

I use the word "see" because the opportunity to open the shop came about so fast. I wasn't sure exactly what I was trying to create. My sign said, SPIRIT RISING, Uplifting Art, Gifts and Services. I wanted people to feel comfortable coming into the shop. I believed art galleries could be intimidating to some people and I wasn't sure how to promote my motivational services, so I figured the best thing was to feature the gifts. I enjoyed surrounding myself with wind chimes, fairy and angel sculptures, artful home decor and inspirational books. Seeing which gifts or books customers liked helped me to strike up conversations with them about the motivational programs that I offered at the shop. My goal became to help each person who came in to feel better about themselves when they left.

**Peace Pilgrim**

By February, more people were coming into the shop, but overall the traffic was still quite slow. I was getting nervous about making enough money to sustain myself. One day when I was particularly overwhelmed with my financial responsibilities, I took a long walk. While walking, I remembered reading about a woman who called herself Peace Pilgrim. From 1953 to 1981, she walked over 25,000 miles on a personal pilgrimage for peace. She walked until given shelter and fasted until given food. In those twenty-eight years, she touched the hearts and minds of thousands of people across North America. Reading about her life had a profound effect on me.

As I walked, I imagined what it would be like to have no possessions or responsibilities; to walk through life with no particular destination or deadline. I pretended I was just passing through the neighborhood and didn't know anyone or anything about the area. Although I was walking streets I had walked many times before, it felt as though I was seeing everything for the first time. I suddenly realized that that was how it felt to be present *in the moment*. I returned home more relaxed, refreshed, and with a clearer mind. After that day, I often felt connected to Peace Pilgrim's spirit when I walked. A year later when someone read an essay I wrote on world peace, he asked if I had been channeling Peace Pilgrim when I wrote it. Perhaps I had.

**John Denver**

I would be remiss if I didn't share yet another story of a spirit that I felt was watching over me. John Denver was one of my very favorite singer/songwriters. His passion for life, for sharing what he believed in through song, and his deep communion with nature touched my heart deeply. I always felt an extremely strong connection to him. Years ago, when I had my first passport photo taken, I was stunned to see how much I looked like him. Many times I have been told that I remind people of John. My mother even said that he was like my twin and a psychic picked up on John's spirit connecting with mine during a card reading. In one of his concerts the cameras show a close-up view of John singing, "Sunshine on My Shoulders." He was looking directly into the camera. I felt as though he was singing directly to me. Even now as I write, I feel his spirit around me so strongly that I have to stop and compose myself. And I know without a doubt that he's telling me to let my spirit soar.

## Power Struggle

I wish I could say I was letting my spirit soar in March of that year. I thought I was doing so well. There I was with a new shop. I was beginning to book public speaking engagements and people were signing up for my seminars in increasing numbers. In many ways, I had begun to claim my power. But it wasn't until I visited my art studio one Saturday that I realized just how much of myself I was still giving away.

In January, I had surprised even myself by inviting an artist I knew from long ago to share my studio space. I had never even *seen* her artwork. I just knew I liked her energy and felt we could work well together. I was also relieved to have someone split the rent with me. I was recovering from an illness on the day she moved in. I sat and watched her bring in her artwork. It was larger and bolder than mine, but had an earthy feel that seemed to go with my work. I had very little of my own art left in the studio. Most of my paintings were now decorating the walls of my shop. Too exhausted to care, I went home and crawled into bed, leaving my friend to divide up and redecorate the studio.

When I brought my paintings to my shop, I was excited about all the extra space left in my studio. Now I could dance with wild abandon as I made big, splashy artwork. I was giddy with anticipation about painting larger and freer than ever before. The problem was I had no time. Every second of my day was consumed with running the shop. I was only going to the studio one day a week and, once there, I was too tired to be able to create much of anything. Gradually, I let my studio mate take over nearly the entire space. As I saw the walls fill up with her big, bold, beautiful work, I became furious, not with her, but with myself for living small. By not even preserving half the wall area, I allowed myself to be robbed of the coveted space I needed to create and display new work.

Many times, as Mary and I decorated the shop together, she would comment that I created my signs and displays on a very small scale. She would say, "This is *your* shop to do with as you please. What is holding you back? Enjoy it!" What she said was true about my life as well. I needed to stop playing small. It was time to shout who I was from the rooftops.

One way I wanted to do that was to finish writing this book. I was receiving strong guidance to do so. The most notable example came from a book Mary picked up for me to read. It was *Medicine Woman* by Lynn V. Andrews. Although I had trouble relating to some of the story, I still felt compelled to finish it. The reason for my compulsion wasn't answered until the very last page. The main character was told by another woman, ". . . I am telling you to give the spirit world to your people. Let your message fly . . . You've seen a lot, you know a lot; but that's not enough . . . Go write a book and give away what you have learned."

One thing I learned was that the nurturing space I created in my shop had a very powerful impact on people. My favorite comment came during an exchange between three customers. Two young women had come in for the first time and another regular customer told them as he was leaving, "This is a very empowering place. You'll find what you need here."

Even though the shop was gradually doing better, the financial risk was still weighing heavily on me. I often wondered if I was foolish to have opened it. I began to lighten up on myself after watching a movie called "Tuck Everlasting." It was about a family of four who unknowingly drink from a fountain of eternal youth. A young woman accidentally stumbles upon them in her travels and learns the secret that they are immortal. The father of the family sits her down for a talk. His words stuck in my mind like glue. He warns her, "Don't be afraid of death. Be afraid of an unlived life." Well, at least I was taking chances, no matter how misguided they might have been. Opening the shop was a step towards trying to live my life, but I felt I still had a long way to go.

The dream I had the following morning was further confirmation. I dreamed I was swimming down river. When I realized there was a waterfall up ahead, I panicked and swam off to the side just in time to keep from going over it. My dream book, *Remembering and Understanding Your Dreams*, says that a waterfall represents "Exuberance and an uninhibited outpouring of creating energy . . . celebrating life." For all the risks I had taken, I still felt that I had not reached that level of exuberant and uninhibited living that I desired. I was afraid to go over the waterfall.

Inhibited or not, I was often reminded that the angels were right there with me at the shop. They made it very clear one morning when I went outside to hang some vinyl lettering in my front window. I had drawn out a paper grid with all the words I wanted to use to describe what we offered in the store. As I was working, the wind blew the packages of lettering and the grid out of my hands. I was able to retrieve the letters but I couldn't find the grid. I finished placing all the words on the window except one. Then I said out loud, "OK angels, I need your help. I can't remember what the last word is." A minute later, a neighbor came around the corner with the paper grid in her hand and asked if it was mine. I thanked her and looked at the list. The word I had forgotten was *angels*.

**Jury Duty**

I think the angels were guiding me a few days later at the courthouse where I had been summoned for jury duty. A questionnaire that I had to fill out asked if there was any reason why I felt I should not be impaneled to hear a trial. I wrote, "With all due respect, I do not feel that it is my personal role to sit in judgment of anyone." I wasn't trying to be smart or get out of jury duty. I was completely calm and prepared to do whatever the court decided. I simply stated my belief and waited to see what would happen.

Initially, I was one of seven people chosen for the jury for an assault case. I was called up to the bench and asked to elaborate on my statement. I explained that it was my spiritual belief that it was not up to me to judge another's actions. I agreed that, yes, I could do it, but that I preferred not to. The judge asked me to take my place back in the jury box, but a few minutes later he asked me to step down and replaced me with someone else. That experience provided me an opportunity to see how I could stay true to myself in a peaceful, loving way. I would have been okay with hearing the case if I had to, but I was quite pleased to be released to live life more in line with my beliefs.

**Breakdown to Breakthrough**

Mid-May found me depressed. As hard as I tried, I was having trouble maintaining my optimism about the shop's success. One day while Mary was there, I burst into tears. I had been working hard for the last six months, but many of the motivational programs I was promoting were getting little or no response. Mary suggested that maybe I needed to let go of them for a while and pursue something else instead. She asked about the possibility of moving my art studio from Western Avenue into the smaller room in my shop. I felt a huge sense of relief at the idea of saving hundreds of dollars each month on studio rent. I gave my studio mate fair notice I was leaving and immediately started transferring my art supplies to the shop. If I still found myself worrying over finances, I would just step into my new studio and create something. It helped me to focus on something positive and stay in the moment.

That seemed to be the theme of every book I picked up over the next few days—stay in the moment! I was beginning to understand what that meant. It did not mean that I did not have any idea of where I was headed. It meant making the current step I was taking more important than the ultimate goal. It meant being mindful of whatever I was doing and, more importantly, being mindful of how I was *being*. I saw that when I was fully present in each moment, even tasks that used to seem tedious and mundane became beautiful. I would take a calming breath, slow myself down ever so slightly, and give whatever I was doing my full attention. By completely surrendering to the moment, I felt a new sense of aliveness and a deeper connection to everyone and everything.

## A Brighter Outlook

In my new, more expanded state of mind, I felt like I was standing on the edge of a cliff ready to fly. I knew I had to keep believing in myself and in my dreams. I became ever more vigilant to only keep optimistic thoughts in my mind. I couldn't afford, figuratively or literally, to let fearful thoughts weigh me down and block good from coming to me. I became daring and put two huge signs in my shop windows that said, "If there were dreams for sale, what would you buy?" and, "I am living my dream. You can too!" More than anything, I wanted to help people believe in themselves and pursue their own dreams.

When appropriate, I would engage my customers in a conversation about their dreams. Often, I would give them a small journal and encourage them to begin writing about their dream as if it already existed. I would say, "Don't worry about how or when or *if* it will come true. All you have to do is imagine your dream in vivid detail with deep emotion and passion. Then let the universe help it unfold in a way that will serve everyone." Each time I helped someone believe in their creative power, I bolstered my own.

## Infinite Possibilities

One morning, after a particularly restful sleep, I revisited in my mind what it was I had actually set out to do with my life. I had recently reconnected with my excitement for doing artwork and I was making headway on writing my book, but what I most wanted to do was motivational speaking. I was just bursting with enthusiasm to share what I had learned about what magnificent co-creators we are and how we really *can* live the life of our dreams. That was the element that was still missing. I was speaking to some individuals who visited the shop, but I pictured myself speaking to much larger audiences. Spontaneously, right there in my kitchen, I recited out loud what I would say to a larger audience.

*"Good morning,"* my voice boomed. *"We live in a world of infinite possibilities. In fact, we* are *infinite possibility! We are individual expressions of the Source that created us. And that Source, some would call it God, is a powerful creator. It can create anything! Since we are expressions of that source, we can create anything! What does that leave out? Nothing! So if this is true, why are we not creating what we want? Because, we don't believe it is possible. Our own disbelief and feelings of unworthiness are the main things blocking us from*

*creating the life of our dreams. Who are we to deserve having everything that our heart desires?*

*"We are the glorious children of God. It is our birthright to have a happy, healthy, meaningful and abundant life. It is literally what we came here to experience – the glory of who we really are. But the glory of who we are scares us to death. It feels much safer to live small, insignificant lives than to accept our responsibility as co-creators and discover how grand we truly are. It is time for us to remember who we are and live the life we came here to live. That's what I want to talk to you about this morning—how to create the life of your dreams."*

I could have spoken for much longer, but I needed to get ready for work. A few minutes later I felt moved to pick up my daily inspiration book. The message was about trusting the universe to support my dream, *even if I couldn't yet see how it could happen!* That was the key – trust.

## Gaining Clarity

I opened the store in the hope of lifting other people's spirits, but I came to realize that the spirit most in need of lifting was my own. There I was aching to tell other people how to live *their* dream, knowing full well that I wasn't completely living my own.

It was time to follow my own advice. One night in late September, I pulled out a book I had read called

*The Circle*, by Laura Day. "The Circle," as she calls it, is about getting clear on what you are wishing for and then having the experience of feeling like it already exists. Hmmm. Had I heard those words before? In my circle, I wrote, *I wish to earn all the money I want while doing what I love to do.* This begged the question, What DID I love to do?

That night I sat down and listed what I did and did not want. I understood the importance of not focusing on the *don't wants,* but I at least needed to know what they were before I could rephrase them positively and manifest any real change. When I was honest with myself, I discovered that I still wanted the same thing I had wanted since long before opening a shop ever entered my mind. I wanted to create art, write my book, and do motivational speaking.

**Closing the Shop**

It was becoming clearer that I needed to close the shop. That thought brought me much relief because of the increasing financial burden, but I didn't know what my next step would be.

Initially, I had believed that I couldn't succeed by just offering my art and motivational services. I had opened the shop and given my art and services second billing to the gifts. I justified this by telling myself that the gifts would make people feel comfortable to come in the shop. Then I would be able to introduce them to my "real work" once they came inside. It was toward the end of my stay there that a good friend suggested that *I* was the one who needed to feel safe by having a gift shop. Then, if it failed, I could blame it on the bad economy instead of bearing the personal defeat I risked by showing my true self, my spiritual work, to the world. Her words were truer than I cared to admit.

Ironically, while I was hiding behind the gift shop, I discovered that most of my return clients came back to enjoy uplifting conversation in the peaceful, nurturing space that I had created. They weren't there for the gifts at all! During the last week the shop was open, I was overrun with people who came in looking for consolation and advice. Once we talked, each one seemed to leave in a much happier state of mind. After the last person left, the song "Suddenly I See" by KT Tunstall came on the radio. I found myself joyfully dancing around the shop to her catchy tune, smiling because suddenly I *did* see what was important to me. It did not have anything to do with selling gifts.

The shop closed at 5pm on Halloween night. Now, I needed to decide how I would use my free time. I started by redecorating my apartment with artwork and small furnishings that I took home from the shop. Someone who had done a card for me commented that the shop felt more like home to me than my home did. It did. I loved how the shop was decorated! By the time I finished incorporating the shop items into my home, I felt as if I had moved to a whole new place. I was ready for a new chapter in my life.

## Mr. Magorium

Two weeks before I closed the shop, I saw the movie, *Mr Magorium's Wonder Emporium.* The story is about a young woman named Mollie who manages a magical toy store that is owned and operated by the eccentric, 243-year-old Mr. Magorium, brilliantly played by Dustin Hoffman. Mollie finds herself at a crossroad when she sees a subway advertisement that asks, *Do you have sparkle?* After she tells Mr. Magorium that she feels stuck in her life, he decides to exit the world and leave the toy store to Mollie. But, the magic that animates the toys in the store is dependent on the owner's state of mind. Mollie doesn't believe that she has any magic of her own, so the toys start to malfunction and the store becomes dark and dreary. During an emotional scene when she is despondent over her boss leaving and fearful of being unable to run the store alone, her boss lovingly tells her, "Your life is an occasion. Rise to it."

Mollie is still overwhelmed with the whole situation. She chooses to put the toy store up for sale, but through a delightful series of events, she eventually finds her "sparkle" and is able to orchestrate all the toys back to life. When I first saw that Mollie kept the store open, I wondered if I was being shown that it was a mistake to close mine. By the end of the movie, I understood the real message: It was time for me to rise to the occasion of my own life and believe in my own magic. I needed to go out and share who I was with the world in a grander, more authentic way.

# 2010—Defining Moments

### Hiding Again

A new friend asked me what I would do next. When I spoke about my motivational work, she asked if I thought I could work from home instead of needing to create another "place" for people to come to. I told her that I could, but within three weeks I found myself looking at another space for rent at the end of my street.

Mary was the one who told me it was available. The space was convenient to my house and she kept saying what a great opportunity it was. I wasn't so sure, but once again I didn't listen to my heart. Just as I had minimized and disregarded the overwhelming fear I had about financing the shop, there was a heavy feeling of *here I go again* about this venture that I also chose to ignore. I kept telling myself that it *was* a great opportunity to continue my motivational work in a place close to home with much more affordable rent.

What I neglected to see was that it was only a great opportunity if that's what *I* really wanted.

As another dear friend once said, "Sometimes synchronicity is the universe's way of saying, *Here is an opportunity for you to choose again.*" I still didn't get it. I thought that synchronicity was *always* a signal to continue moving forward in the direction I was currently headed. It never occurred to me that it might be a signal to pay attention to what I was creating and ask myself if that's what I wanted.

For years, whenever anyone suggested that I would someday own my own gallery or shop, I would always say that I had no interest in being tied down to one location. So why was I doing this all over again? Part of it was the intrigue of decorating another place. I really enjoyed doing that. Partly, it was my somewhat misguided faith in synchronicity. But, mostly, it was that I had let someone else's opinion of what was best for me overpower my own. To complicate matters further, I decided that I needed help, so I recruited four other people, including Mary, to join me. Together we tried to create a healing center, but just like in the shop, I became more focused on creating the space than on the work I planned to do there.

Fear was holding me back, fear of failure *and* my fear of success. Many times over the years I remembered people telling me that I would someday be rich and famous. As nice as that sounded, I wasn't sure I knew how to handle either one. And I certainly didn't think I knew how to handle the technological end of a successful business venture, so it was easier to keep playing small.

We moved into the building on the first of January, 2010. By mid-February, I was already finding it difficult to work with the group. For reasons I did not understand, many of my old insecurities kept resurfacing. I kept second guessing myself in almost everything I did. It was important to make sure the group was in agreement with my decisions, but I seemed to be taking the need for approval to an extreme. I thought the difficulty I had working with the group was a sign that I needed to tame my ego and deal with my insecurities, but the harder I tried to make it work, the more miserable I felt. Trying to *fit in*, I even considered giving up the Spirit Rising name that I had worked so hard to promote.

I was sensing Roger's presence quite often around this time. I interpreted this as his support. Another friend, who had known my husband well, suggested I was sensing him around because he was worried about me. She said he had been worried about me ever since I moved out on my own and, now that I was struggling, he was making his presence known again. She also helped me see that I was losing my way and that was why I couldn't make this venture work. "You know," she said, "in all the years I've known you, I have never once heard you say that you wanted to open a gift shop or healing center."

She was right. I had pursued both of those ventures out of fear that what I already had to offer the world wasn't enough. What I *did* learn from them and my art studio was that I was very good at creating healing spaces, both physically and psychologically. Over and over again, people told me how safe and comforted they felt around me. The location didn't matter. I needed to believe in myself and the gifts I had to offer the world. And wasn't that what Spirit Rising was all about?! I had just been dealt a huge lesson about the very thing I most wanted to teach. It was time for me to stop acting in other people's plays and begin starring in my own.

Following my friend's visit, I took the necessary steps to separate myself from the group at the healing center. Once I realized what I had been doing, making the decision was quick and easy. Making the announcement was not. I was the one who had originally formed and inspired the group. We were already six months into the venture. This most certainly would not be a popular decision. But, if there was one thing I *had* learned over the years, it was this: With each decision I made, it was very important to ask myself if I was acting out of fear or love. In this case, I needed to know if I was running away from something difficult that I needed to learn from, or if I was running *toward* something that was more in line with my personal truth and soul purpose. If I was running away, it would likely be a poor decision for myself and the group. If I was running toward inner joy and my true path, the decision would be for the highest good of everyone involved, no matter how disruptive it appeared at the time. It was not for me to know how anyone else's path should unfold. My job was to stay true to my inner guidance in the most loving way possible.

I wish I could say that I succeeded in doing that all of the time. There were times I let my fear get in the way and I know my words were sometimes less than kind. But, every day while meditating, I practiced sending love to each person in the group. I pictured their faces lit up with joy and inner peace because that is what I truly wished for each of them. For myself, I finally acknowledged that I was a life coach, inspirational artist and speaker and began marketing myself that way under the Spirit Rising name.

**A Mister Rogers Moment**

Although I was blessed with many interests and was often praised for what people called my many "talents," I was still struggling to find a way to combine them into a cohesive whole. I often envied those who offered just one service. They seemed sure of themselves and of their direction much earlier in life than I did. At the age of sixty, I was still trying to define myself.

A few years earlier, a good friend gave me a copy of *Life's Journeys According to Mister Rogers* by Fred Rogers, the well-known children's television show host. In it, he spoke about how whole he felt when, later in life, he discovered that he could combine and use every one of his talents in the service of children through his show. He said, "I can tell you that it was that particular focus that made all the difference for me. I can also tell you that the directions weren't written on the back of my college diploma. They came ever so slowly for me; and ever so firmly. I trusted that they would emerge. All I can say is it's worth the struggle to discover who you really are and how you, in your own way, can put life together as something that means a lot to you. It's a miracle when you finally discover whom you're best equipped to serve – and we're all equipped to serve in some way."

I craved a moment of clarity about why I was here in the world in this particular body with these particular interests. How could I serve in a way that was meaningful to me? I read and re-read that passage many times. I did my best to trust that the answer would come . . . and I waited.

Part of the answer came to me through the very same person who gave me that book. On this particular night, she was reviewing the new brochure I had put together. She said it lacked focus and was too confusing. I had to agree with her, but I didn't know what to do about it. She suggested that I concentrate on marketing just one thing. When I had trouble choosing, she pointed out that many of the workshops I had offered in the past included elements of all my other interests and that, if I thought about that, I might even have a "Mister Rogers moment."

The following morning, as I worked on a new brochure, everything fell into place. I could see how each of my passions *were* already elements of my workshops and that they all revolved around empowering people to live a more fulfilling life. I could feature my art, writing, speaking and life coaching skills without having to credential each one separately. I could simply say, "I give empowerment workshops." Wow! It was astonishingly simple and instantly made me think of the title of one of my favorite books by Alan Cohen called, *I Had it All the Time.*

# Harvest

## 2011—Entitled to Miracles

**Only Dreaming?**

I was ready to offer empowerment workshops to help people live a better life, but the question was, "What constitutes a better life?" I knew I wanted to help people find more joy and meaning in their lives, but just like all those years ago, it still felt like something was missing, not just from my workshop curriculum, but from my life.

With more free time, I found myself re-reading a book I had discovered a few years earlier. I hadn't been quite ready to hear its message back then. This time it catapulted me into a whole new world almost overnight. The author's message was so unconventional that it shook the foundation of everything I believed up to that point. It also made perfect sense.

*The Disappearance of the Universe,* by Gary Renard, had my full attention. Its message, as I understood it, didn't speak of how to improve my earthly life, though that is what happened when I embraced its teachings. Instead, it opened my eyes to the possibility of completely *transcending* the entire cycle of birth and death by recognizing my true identity as One with God. I learned that God is pure love and *only* pure love. Being love, He could *never* create, condone, or even entertain an awareness of the suffering we often experience as human beings. He *did*, however, create *us*, in His image, as wholly loving creators with unlimited power—including the power to imagine, in extraordinarily vivid detail, what it would be like to be separate from Him.

It is my understanding that, in our natural state as spirit, our initial thought of wondering what it would be like to have a separate identity from God projects us into a dreamlike state that we call *life*, but it is more like a deep sleep and a forgetting of our divine nature. Unconsciously, we are upset with ourselves for thinking we have caused this separation and fearful of retribution from God. We deal with the ensuing guilt by projecting the blame out onto other bodies in our dream. We see *them* as the cause of all our problems. In truth, we aren't really guilty of anything except a mistaken idea about ourselves and others. We could never really be separate from what we are. It is through forgiving others that we are able to forgive that unconscious part of ourselves. We begin to heal and experience the truth of our Oneness with God.

**A Course in Miracles**

Gary Renard's book is a supplemental teaching guide to *A Course in Miracles*, which is a modern spiritual guidebook. Reading his book prompted me to begin studying *A Course in Miracles* in earnest on January 1, 2011. The *Course* is unwavering in its pure and simple message:

> "Nothing real can be threatened.
> Nothing unreal exists.
> Herein lies the peace of God."

It is a self-study course that includes 365 workbook lessons, a textbook, and a manual for teachers. The lengthy text gradually introduces, and then continually repeats and expands upon, its teachings. Along with the daily lessons, it helps the reader slowly and gently awaken from their dream of separation from God to an unquestioning, unshakable knowing of their complete Oneness with Him.

At the time I began re-reading Gary's book, there was already a tremendous amount of change happening in my outer life. It was *nothing* compared to the change that was occurring inside my mind. I seemed to be moving forward at warp speed into new territory with no idea where it would take me. Having my spiritual beliefs challenged was particularly disconcerting because I was soon scheduled to present a series of five motivational workshops at the hospital where I had been employed years ago. I no longer had a clue what I was going to say. I was aching to begin talking about what I was learning from the *Course*, but I didn't yet know how to articulate these new and challenging ideas.

As it turned out, the majority of my speaking opportunities were cancelled for various reasons. Although part of me was disappointed, mostly I was relieved. I needed more time to assimilate these new ideas and practice the forgiveness that was such a huge part of the *Course*'s message. My first lesson was to forgive the people and circumstances that led to so many of my workshops being cancelled. I thought that all of those speaking opportunities would not have presented themselves unless the timing was right for what I had to say. Apparently, it wasn't. So, I trusted that the answers would eventually reveal themselves. I kept reciting a passage from the "Manual for Teachers" that says:

*"I am here only to be truly helpful.*
*I am here to represent Him Who sent me.*
*I do not have to worry about what to say or what to do,*
*because He Who sent me will direct me.*
*I am content to be wherever He wishes, knowing He goes*
*there with me.*
*I will be healed as I let Him teach me to heal."*

I have used the word "ideas" to describe what I was learning, but it was really more like a remembering of a truth that I had always known, but just forgotten. I was remembering that only love is real. It has no opposite. Everything else is merely an illusion, an idea in the mind of man that we are somehow separate from God. That fearful thought shows up in many forms: worry, anger, hate, jealousy, and so on. None of them are real. Whenever I experienced them, I tried to remember to ask for help to see the situation from a higher perspective. I asked for help in forgiving the illusion I had created that made me want to blame others. I asked to see only God (Love) in everyone and everything. If people weren't extending love, then I tried to remember that they must be *calling* for love. Challenging as it was, I knew it was a practice of great importance. The less I resisted life and the more I embraced each moment as a divine opportunity to forgive and to extend love, instead of blaming or trying to *get* love, the more beautiful life became.

## It's All You

As I woke up to the fact that I was only dreaming, I realized that we are all parts of each other's dreams. If I judged someone else, I was really judging a part of myself. Likewise, if I loved and forgave them, I was loving and forgiving myself! This helped me to remember that I was *not* a victim. I was a divine, loving Being and joyful co-creator with God.

I realized that my *only* purpose for being here in this body was to remember this truth about myself and share it with the world. And the joyful truth is that I am One with God (Love) and therefore entitled to miracles. My favorite quote, by Macrina Wiederkehr, became, "Oh God, please help me to believe the truth about myself, no matter how beautiful it is." Remembering the truth meant forgiving the world I had mentally created and seeing everyone and everything through the miraculous eyes of love. I was learning to see past the illusion and experience the love within each person whether they were being lovable or not. *That* was the miracle.

I was also learning that I couldn't see the truth if I was focused on the future or the past. I had to let go of all grievances and expectations. A grievance is a belief that something, seemingly outside myself, needs to change in order for me to be happy. An expectation is a future grievance that something, again outside myself, needs to happen a certain way in order for me to be at peace. Grievances tie me to the past and expectations tie me to the future and both deny me the happiness and peace that are available right now. They prevent me from waking to the fact that I am dreaming and that my true state of joy is available not only *now,* but *forever.*

**New Pathways**

The more excited I became about what I was learning, the more I found myself wanting to share these ideas with others. A friend encouraged me to offer a spiritual discussion group in my home twice a month, which helped me connect with many wonderful people. Later, I also began facilitating a *Course in Miracles* discussion group which was, and still is, tremendously helpful to me. Another opportunity presented itself when my friend Kathy offered to create a blog for me. I decided to post a weekly *Thought from SPIRIT RISING*. I dedicated the blog to, "Helping us return to joy." Before long, I had a small but enthusiastic following. It was a conversation with Kathy about my blog entries that also led me to another consideration.

About nine months earlier, I had researched the possibility of becoming a non-denominational minister. I was told that the title would provide legal backing for me to work as a life coach/spiritual counselor, but becoming ordained simply for that reason did not feel right. I decided to wait. Later, when Kathy suggested that many of my blog entries had a sermon-like quality to them and asked if I had ever considered becoming a minister, the idea resonated with me in a deeper way. I searched the web, trying to locate the website I had remembered liking nine months ago, but to no avail. During my search, I came across a site that offered courses based on *A Course in Miracles*. That immediately got my attention, especially when I discovered that I could be ordained through this spiritual college. Whether I decided to go that far in my studies or not, I knew I wanted to experience those facilitated correspondence courses for myself. I immediately ordered the first five of twenty-two.

## Do You Want It?

Around the same time, I had lunch with another new friend who is a very gifted psychic. Although I wasn't there for a reading, at one point in our conversation she felt compelled to share a vision with me of what she saw possible in my future. She had my full attention as she described in great detail the vision I have had for myself for a long time.

She spoke of me moving to a place in the country with lots of land and a loft, or perhaps a barn, where I would have a large art studio. There was also a large, welcoming space where people could come for spiritual gatherings and ceremonies, maybe even small weddings. She said I would be very peaceful and happy there. I laughed when she said that I would be like "the grandest of earth mothers" there. I was very excited about this unexpected turn of events. She had taken my fantasy and helped me to believe it was possible. Three or four times, though, she stopped talking, pointed at me and said, "Do you want it? Because I can see you having it if you want it! Do you want it?"

I knew this was an important question because, in the past, I had manifested the shop which, in spite of all its good points, was often very stressful and left me deeply in debt. Then I manifested the healing center that, in spite of the fine people I worked with, greatly magnified my stress, leaving me emotionally depleted! I believe I created those two situations partly because I felt that what I already had to offer was inadequate, but also because I bought into someone else's idea of what my dream should be instead of listening to my own heart. Now, here I was, being told that my vision could come true. I was excited, yes. But this time I would make sure that the dream I lived was completely my *own*.

## Admissions

My new friend and I also talked about our career paths. There were many parallels, including the dilemma of what to call ourselves to define the type of work we did. My friend said that she had begun calling herself a spiritual counselor. I had never put those two words together when describing my work, but I instantly recognized that spiritual counseling was exactly what I was doing. After all the different guises, I was finally ready to announce to the world that I was a spiritual counselor, writer, speaker and artist. Under the business name of Spirit Rising, I had been counseling, speaking, writing and painting for years. Ironically, the only thing missing was the admission that I was allowing myself to be led by spirit!

I felt that I had to *admit* to a spiritual path because it terrified me. I never understood where that deep-seated fear came from, but admitting to my husband that I was on a spiritual path was something I simply could not do. That is why I so desperately needed to be on my own. I needed to fully explore my spirituality, and I did not feel comfortable doing that with him. Hiding the books I was reading when he pulled into our driveway was one of my first clues that our marriage was in trouble. I think part of the reason I was so fearful was because I was surrounded by family members who, I believed, held no interest or respect for a spiritual path. My husband and sons were very scientifically oriented. My brother and his family were as well. Also, due to losing her own mother at an early age, my mother had renounced any and all religions and spirituality long ago. The only person who I thought might have been spiritually inclined was my dad and he had passed on. In their defense, I don't think my family would have judged me nearly as harshly as I imagined they would, if at all. My husband, of all people, had always encouraged me to be my own person and respected my choices in life. He probably would have lovingly supported me no matter what path I took, but I never gave him the chance.

As a result, when I entered my relationship with Johnny, I vowed to myself that I would always be honest with him about my spirituality. But as my commitment to a spiritual path grew to the point that I was considering ordination, I worried if it would come between us. I caught myself trying to minimize or cover up my new direction. Red flag! Red flag! I was not going down *that* road again! So I began sharing my new beliefs with him and including him in what I was doing. I had to give us the chance that Roger and I never had.

**Patterns**

I recognized other patterns in my life as well. I saw how I had given my power away many times by relying too heavily on other people's opinions and advice. It would be a few more months before I would recognize the most self-destructive pattern of all.

It was a very busy time in my life. I had made the decision to sell the house that Roger and I had owned together. Because neither of us had re-married, it was still in my name. Our son, Greg, lived there for a few years after Roger passed. After he moved out, I chose to stay in the apartment that I had long ago made my home and put the house up for sale. Johnny and I were fixing up the house during his weekend visits with me. It had endured years of neglect during our divorce and after my husband died and needed a tremendous amount of work. I was amazed as I watched Johnny repair things in room after room. Starting in mid-June, we put in 16 to 24 hours of hard labor each weekend for seven weeks to get it ready for the first open house. With an incredibly low budget, he so transformed the house that I was able to double my asking price!

During that time, even though my new psychic friend had described my dream life to me, I still felt that my life was a bit directionless. When I would ask myself what it was I wanted, I realized that I really didn't know what would be best for me. So, I stopped trying to figure it all out and surrendered everything to God. Throughout the day I would silently pray, *Thank you for the perfect home, job, income and partners for my life's purpose, whatever that is.* Then one day it dawned on me that I already *had* the perfect house; that fixing it up was the perfect job which would provide me with the perfect income and Johnny was my perfect partner! I dove into the renovation process with renewed enthusiasm. Just two days after the first open house in August, we had an offer. By late October the house was sold.

At the same time that we were finishing work on the house, I was also planning an eight-day trip to the Pacific Northwest with two girlfriends. Not having had much chance to travel, the trip was a big deal to me. And, if planning for my trip and trying to sell the house at the same time wasn't enough excitement, I was unexpectedly invited to interview for a fantastic job. I wasn't looking for a job. But the house repairs were almost done and here was this new offer, which came just a few days before I was leaving for my trip. I wasn't sure what to do. I decided to explore the opportunity before I left for my trip, but not make a decision until I returned.

In between the first and second job interviews, I went on my trip to the Pacific Northwest. For months I had sensed that I would be going on a life-changing trip. I assumed it was a trip to Wyoming to visit Michael and Leslie in their new home. When those plans unexpectedly fell through, I was bewildered. But, the very next day a friend mentioned that she and her girlfriend were planning a trip to Oregon. She said, "God told me to invite you to come along." Who can refuse an invitation like *that*?

The itinerary for the trip was already planned. This worked in nicely with my new plan of surrendering everything to God. This trip would be the perfect time to practice. So, I declared to them and myself that I was "just along for the ride." I had never traveled anywhere without my family and without having a great amount of input in the planning. I was really excited at the opportunity to sit back and see where each day would take me. I was ready to let go.

The trip to Oregon was extraordinary. We spent four nights in Portland, exploring the city and visiting with my friend's daughters. An afternoon spent touring the Japanese Garden was the highlight of those four days. My one secret wish was that I could have more time to spend there on my own, without being part of a tour group. To my delight, a change in plans gave me that opportunity the very next day.

From Portland, we traveled up through Seattle, Washington to San Juan Island. I could hardly wait to get there. My idea of the perfect vacation had always been to see exquisite scenery and spend time alone in a beautiful, natural setting with God. That's what this trip promised. The scenery on the ferry ride alone was astounding. I spent most of the time on the bow of the boat, braving the fierce cold so I could have an unimpeded view of the snow capped mountains. Standing out there, with the sun on my face and the wind in my hair, I felt my spirit expanding in all directions.

The following morning, I had the opportunity to spend a lot of time on a very remote part of the island, surrounded by the most serene beauty I had ever experienced. I slid my way down an extremely steep slope to a beach of ultra-fine white sand. The water, smooth and motionless, mirrored the surrounding mountains. I sat on one of the many pieces of driftwood that filled the cove, trying to inhale the peace and serenity to take back with me. I was so captivated with the scenery that it took me a while to even notice that I had moved down to sit in the sand and buried my bare feet deep in the cool earth. I just wanted to completely merge with my surroundings. I have no idea how long I sat there transfixed. It seemed like it was just me and

God. Overwhelmed, I wept with joy. I felt as though my entire life had led me to that moment of deep connection with the Divine.

On our way back to Seattle, we took another spectacular ferry ride to Port Townsend to visit my friend's former roommate. We only had about an hour to explore the island before we met up with her. She wanted us to come to her home for tea and dessert. My initial thought was that I didn't want to *waste* my time sitting in someone's house when there was a whole island to explore. But, then I remembered that I was just along for the ride and that I needed to trust where I was being led.

Our hostess was delightful, but it wasn't until we were settled outside on her patio, sipping tea, that the realization of why we were there struck me. Her house was EXACTLY like the house I had imagined myself living in in the near future. It had natural wood siding with tomato red trim, criss-crosses in the windows and a pot of red geraniums outside the arched front door. Inside, there was a vaulted ceiling in the main living area that exposed a hand-railed walkway around the perimeter of the second floor with bedrooms off of it. Outside, there was a separate building for her art studio; another building used as a guest cottage, *and* she kept her horse just down the street at a beautiful stable with a gorgeous view of the mountains! If I had objected to going to her house for tea, I would have missed out on the most incredible lesson of the entire trip. Dreams really *can* come true! In that moment I knew for sure that if I could see my entire dream laid out before me *there* on the other side of the country, I knew I could manifest it for myself anywhere.

I had come for the scenery, but I left with so much more. I had already manifested many wonderful things in my life, but I was still putting limits on what I thought was possible. Now, I felt invincible! Through that trip, I received the gift of renewed hope that I could truly live the life of my dreams. So, I had to smile when we arrived at the Seattle airport for our return flight. My *Angel Numbers 101* book says that the number 555 means that, "Huge changes are rumbling throughout your entire life!" At the airport, we parked in space number 55, the odometer read 555 miles, and the temperature was 55 degrees. I didn't even begrudge returning home. I felt that an exciting new life lay at my feet. It was mine for the taking and I was ready.

My first order of business was the potential new job. The choice seemed very difficult until a wise friend advised me to be still and ask myself what was this situation *for*. Why did an incredible employment opportunity show up now, just as I was coming into enough money from the sale of the house and free time to pursue my speaking, writing and art? Would it lead me in some wonderful yet unknown direction or was it a test of my resolve to believe in myself and follow my heart?

For days I agonized over the decision. I listened to the rather forceful advice of many well- intentioned friends to take the position. I almost convinced myself that they were right. But, during my second interview, every time I envisioned saying yes to the job, I saw myself choking on the words. Then an amazing thing happened. The company owner asked me to tell him more about an upcoming seminar I was scheduled to present called "Return to Joy." When I finished speaking he got very quiet. Then he said, "I can hear the intensity and passion in your voice as you speak of your work. I'm concerned," he continued, "that, if I offer you this job, you will soon become angry about being taken away from the work you are already doing."A wave of clarity jolted through me. This was not an opportunity. It was a test; a test that I had failed many times before! If I took the job, it would be out of fear; fear that my friends knew better than I did what was best for me; fear that what I was already doing wasn't good enough; and fear that I couldn't enjoy an abundant life doing what I loved to do.

And *that* was the pattern. *Detour and self-sabotage!* I was doing things for all the wrong reasons. I did it when I opened the shop. I did it again when I opened the healing center. I didn't have enough confidence that I could make it on my own as a speaker, writer and artist, so I acted out of fear. I jumped into ventures that actually took all my time and energy *away* from what I really wanted to do.

Here I was at the same crossroads again, finally having the promise of enough money and time to pursue my dream, but having another tempting carrot dangled in front of me. Should I take the lucrative job that promised financial stability and prestige or not?

I quieted my mind and asked for guidance. It soon came to me in rapid succession from many sources. I learned that I was rationalizing that a situation (the job) was okay when it was not; that everything I needed was right in front of me if I would only look. I heard that there was no need to create drama and worry about having enough and that I shouldn't proceed blindly or out of anxiety or fear. I was told that I was a born teacher and my natural counseling abilities would serve me well in a professional way. Most importantly, I was told to trust in God. I was reassured that my passion for certain things, such as speaking, writing and art, was divinely inspired and that divine inspiration comes with divine instructions, and support!

I asked. I listened. But, had I heard? Would I stay true to myself or follow my old, destructive patterns? Everything Spirit Rising stood for, that *I* stood for, was in the balance.

I said, "no" to the job, and, "YES!" to myself.

It was time to choose joy.

# 2012—Choosing Joy

## Saying "Yes"

I finally got it. This was *my* life and I could do whatever I pleased. I would have to deal with the consequences, but no one else was holding the reins but me. My first step in saying "yes" to myself was telling Johnny about my desire to move further away from him to someplace more rural. To my surprise, he said he would look forward to visiting me in a more rural, retreat-like setting, even if it meant a longer commute. I realized that he had always loved and supported me unconditionally. My fear of him not accepting the more spiritual side of me was also unfounded. It didn't matter how seemingly crazy or different my beliefs were—he always kept an open mind. Johnny not only accepted my spirituality, he encouraged it. And, it didn't matter if I moved further away—he would follow. It didn't matter if I dressed crazily and wore feathers in my hair—he loved it. The more authentically I lived, the more Johnny loved me. *I* was the one who had been running away from myself. Not him. I had been running because, as much as I loved Johnny, and as much as he tried to support me, I saw an ever widening gap in our spiritual beliefs and what we wanted from life. I knew things needed to change, and they did. Although we are no longer together, the deep love I have in my heart for him remains.

It was acknowledging and honoring my own spiritual growth that led me away from Johnny, and I was still afraid of what everyone else would think if I spoke the truth about my beliefs, if I wrote a book about my spiritual journey, if I became a minister. Would it cause a rift between us too? It was hardest to be authentic around the people I loved the most. I wanted their acceptance. That was the biggest obstacle to choosing joy for myself. It took me sixty years to learn that it was not *their* acceptance I needed, it was my own.

I had been ministering to people all my life. Ordination was the perfect next step in my journey. Once I accepted that about myself, telling my family about my ministry became easy. My announcement was met with great surprise, but none of the harsh judgment that I had feared. Instead, it led to healing conversations and deeper understanding of each other.

## Joy vs. Happiness

Although I sometimes used the words interchangeably, I was coming to the realization that happiness is not the same as joy. Happiness is associated with happenings, happenstance, luck and fortune. If conditions are favorable, you're happy; if not, you're unhappy. It is a temporary emotion with lots of ups and downs. Joy, on the other hand, is directly related to Spirit and has nothing to do with the physical world. It can only be experienced in this moment and only in your mind. It is an unconditional acceptance of what *is*; a feeling of living in a constant state of grace; a deep inner knowing that all is well, regardless of your circumstances. Joy is not dependent upon, nor can it be affected by, anything outside of you.

I spent over twenty-five years of my life trying to figure out what was missing. What was missing was my joyful, authentic self. I had not yet realized that the joy I was seeking was not in the *world*. The joy was in *me*. It was not something I needed to *get* or be worthy of. It is what I am.

I had fallen into the trap of thinking that certain things had to happen in my life before I could be joyful. I thought that before I could complete this book about joy, I had to have moved into the house of my dreams, secured a great deal of money, become a well-known artist, writer, speaker, and so on. But joy does not come from those external things. Only happiness requires circumstances, including people, to change. Joy requires changing your perception of yourself. You have to realize that you *are* joy. My book and blog, my paintings, my ordination, even my spiritual discussion groups; those were all external steps I took toward choosing joy by living more authentically. But I knew in my heart that what I was *doing* was not as important as how I was *being*.

**Being Joy**

*A Course in Miracles* says, "The world merely represents your thoughts. And it will change entirely as you elect to change your mind, and choose the joy of God as what you really want. Your self is radiant in this holy joy. Unchanged, unchanging, and unchangeable, forever and forever . . . . . Pain is illusion. Joy is reality. Pain is but sleep; joy is awakening. Pain is deception; joy alone is truth." I knew that accepting this would finally set me free.

T.S. Eliot said, "We shall not cease from exploration, and the end of all our exploring will be to arrive where we started and know the place for the first time." The more I heeded the voice of God within me, the more clearly I understood that God's will for me was perfect joy. *He* was not withholding joy from me. *I* was blocking my awareness of the joy I shared with *Him*. The question was not, *How could I get more joy?* The question was, *How much could I handle?*

God is the source of joy, but He is not separate from me. Knowing Him brought me to joy because knowing God meant knowing myself. When I took time to quiet my mind and follow the inner guidance of my higher self, my life became easier and far more joyful. It was not because I was "lucky." It was because I was learning to walk with Spirit. I discovered that it was not my small self (ego) that I needed to trust, it was the voice of God. Guidance from that voice was far different from what the ego would tell me. The ego always made me feel anxious, hurried, worried, angry, jealous, fearful, and so on. Spirit's guidance always made me feel calm, more loving, and peaceful. It was the voice of patience, acceptance and compassion. I finally learned to surrender by admitting that I did not know what was best for me. I did not know what anything was for. Throughout my day I would silently ask, *How should I see this situation? What shall I do now?* I learned to put Spirit in charge.

When I participated in and embraced God's joyful vision for me, I experienced an ever-increasing amount of synchronicity in my life, but with greater insight into how that was happening. Returning to Shirley MacLaine's quote about synchronicity, she said, ". . . we are living and working with Creation . . . Synchronicity is the connecting link that we have to a nonmaterial and nonphysical reality . . ." I finally understood! I was experiencing synchronicity because I was tapping into the universal mind of God, which I am a part of. There was nothing external to myself giving me signs and coordinating my life, because I was not separate from anyone or anything, including God. *I* was creating the synchronicity! Was the number five really significant to me? Yes, but only because I *chose* to make it symbolic. All the signs that I had allowed to guide my life weren't messages *for* me. They were messages *from* me!

And, the message is clear. Love is everywhere, in spite of what my five senses tell me. I cannot fight hate with hatred, but I can dissolve it with love. I can *be* love in all circumstances. Only love is real. Everything else is illusion; a false thought of me being separate from God. It is only by letting go and looking beyond the illusion of this physical world of separation that I can experience being the love, peace and joy that I am. I can see God everywhere, in everyone. Inspirational author Louise Hay says that she starts her day by affirming, "Only good lies before me." As I learned to look past the illusion of the physical world and see everyone and everything through the eyes of love, I started affirming that, "Only *God* lies before me." And, now I realize that only God lies *within* me. Wherever I am, God *is*. And, all is well.

I remember back to the morning I woke up laughing in Sedona. That was the first time I was ever conscious of experiencing joy for joy's sake. I was euphoric; my heart overflowing with gratitude; bursting with love that I wanted to share. For days after my trip I felt giggly, and I was oh-so-easily amused. There was a sense of lightness about me, about everyone and every situation that I had not detected before. It was hard to get upset about anything. Joy just bubbled up from inside of me for no particular reason. Now I understand. I was experiencing my true self.

And when you *are* joy . . . being joyful doesn't need a reason.

# Epilogue

In writing this book, I set out to share my story with others. In the end, I discovered that the writing was for myself. It helped me to better understand the love that I am, why I am here, and how I can best serve the world. I have been able to step into my life with more courage and grace than I ever dreamed possible.

The name Spirit Rising embodies a sense of hope. It celebrates our infinite creative potential and our capacity for ever-expanding joy. It upholds a vision of a happier life that I now know is completely attainable. We are *all* spirit rising. I aim to share this vision with the world. As we awaken to our true nature, we realize an ever-increasing awareness of our capacity to love and be loved. We learn to positively shape our "reality" and to experience oneness with everyone and everything.

For many years I thought Spirit Rising was a name. I believed it was part of my identity. First it was the title of one of my paintings. Then it became the name of my art studio. Later it was the Native American name I chose for myself. I also called my shop Spirit Rising and, more recently, I founded Spirit Rising Ministries. But, like my new understanding of *self*, the meaning of Spirit Rising has also changed. It is no longer about my painting, art studio or ministry, although Spirit Rising is what I choose to call them. It is no longer about this person I call Paula who loves to go to powwows and wear feathers in her hair.

Spirit Rising is not a name. It is a process. It is a journey back to the true essence of what I am; a growing awareness and acceptance of what has always been. *A Course in Miracles* says, "And so the journey which the Son of God began has ended in the light from which he came." I know that my body and the events I experience on earth are temporary. They are merely vehicles that the Holy Spirit uses to help take me home to my realization of Oneness with God. That is where I always have been and always will be. I have not really changed or traveled anywhere. I have simply risen above my own misguided thoughts and perceptions and awakened to the glorious truth about myself. I am One with God in love, peace and joy, eternally. And so are you.

Join me.

We are all journeying toward this truth together.

It is glorious.

It is inevitable.

It is the journey of Spirit Rising.

# CREDITS

## BOOKS

Clark, Mary Higgins. *Daddy's Little Girl.* New York, NY: Simon and Schuster, 2002

Dyer, Wayne W. *10 Secrets of Success.* California: Hay House, Inc., 2001

—. *You'll See it When You Believe It.* New York: W. Morrow, 1989

—. *Your Sacred Self, Making the Decision to be Free.* New York, NY: Harper Collins, 1995

Hamilton-Parker, Craig. *Remembering and Understanding Your Dreams.* New York: Sterling Publishing Company, Inc., 2000

Hay, Louise. *You Can Heal Your Life.* Santa Monica, CA: Hay House, 1984

MacLaine, Shirley. *Sage-ing While Age-ing.* New York, NY: Atria Books, 2007

Palmer, Helen. Story adapted from the Walt Disney motion picture. *So Dear to my Heart.* New York: Simon and Schuster, 1948

Renard, Gary. *The Disappearance of the Universe.* Carlsbad, California: Hay House, Inc., 2002 (The ideas represented herein are the personal interpretation and understanding of the author and are not necessarily endorsed by the copyright holder of *A Course in Miracles.*)

Rogers, Fred. *Life's Journeys According to Mister Rogers.* New York: Hyperion, 2005

Schucman, Helen. *A Course in Miracles.* Glen Ellen, Calif.: Foundation for Inner Peace, 1975 (The ideas represented herein are the personal interpretation and understanding of the author and are not necessarily endorsed by the copyright holder of *A Course in Miracles.*)

Shinn, Florence Scovel. *The Game of Life and How to Play It.* Marina Del Rey: DeVorss & Company, 1925

Stahlmann, Catherine. *Bunny Blue.* Chicago: Rand McNally & Company, 1947

Virtue, Doreen, Ph.D. *Angel Numbers 101.* Carlsbad, CA: Hay House, Inc., 2008

—. *Healing with the Fairies, Oracle Cards.* Carlsbad, CA: Hay House, Inc., 2001 (a positive change-parenting)

—. *Magical Mermaids and Dolphins.* Carlsbad, CA: Hay House, Inc., 200

## SONGS

Bocelli, Andrea / Brightman, Sarah. "Time to Say Goodbye." <u>Romanza</u>, PolyGram Records, 1996.

Hawkins, Sophie B. "As I Lay Me Down." <u>Whaler</u>. Columbia, 1994.

Kelly, Robert. "I Believe I Can Fly." <u>R.</u>, Atlantic, Jive, 1996.

Lennon, John/McCartney, Paul. "Let it Be." <u>Let it Be</u>, Apple Records, 1970.

Lowry, Mark/Greene, Buddy. "Mary Did You Know?" <u>Mary Did You Know?</u> Spring House, 2004.

Rimes, LeAnn. "One Way Ticket." <u>Blue</u>, Curb Records, Inc., 1996.

Savage Garden. "I knew I Loved You." <u>Affirmation</u>, Sony BMG Music Entertainment, 1999.

Simon, Paul. "Father and Daughter." <u>The Essential Paul Simon</u>, Atlantic Records/ATG, 2007.

Tunstall, KT. "Suddenly I See." <u>Eye to the Telescope</u>, Virgin, 2006.

—. "Black Horse and the Cherry Tree." <u>Eye to the Telescope</u>, Virgin, 2005.

**MOVIES**

Helm, Z. (Director.) 2007, *Mr. Magorium's Wonder Emporium.* Los Angeles, CA: 20th Century Fox.

Keller, F. (Director.) 1981, *Tuck Everlasting.* Burbank, CA: Walt Disney Studios.

**POEMS**

Author Unknown. Balloonist's Prayer, believed to have been adapted from an old Irish sailor's prayer

Noyes, Daneen. "Spirit Rising"

**ARTICLES**

Lehr, Dick, "Split Screen", Boston Globe Online/Sunday Magazine, 31, Dec., 1999, http://cache.boston.com/globe/magazine/1-28/featurestory1.shtml.

Made in the USA
Charleston, SC
24 May 2014